Rapid BeagleBoard Prototyping with MATLAB and Simulink

Leverage the power of BeagleBoard to develop and deploy practical embedded projects

Dr Xuewu Dai

Dr Fei Qin

PUBLISHING

BIRMINGHAM - MUMBAI

Rapid BeagleBoard Prototyping with MATLAB and Simulink

First published: October 2013

Production Reference: 1211013

Published by Packt Publishing Ltd.
Livery Place
35 Livery Street
Birmingham B3 2PB, UK.

ISBN 978-1-84969-604-3

www.packtpub.com

Cover Image by Abhishek Pandey (abhishek.pandey1210@gmail.com)

Credits

Authors
Dr Xuewu Dai
Dr Fei Qin

Reviewers
Ezequiel Aceto
Amit Pandurang Karpe

Acquisition Editor
Joanne Fitzpatrick

Commissioning Editor
Mohammed Fahad

Technical Editors
Menza Mathew
Rohit Kumar Singh

Project Coordinator
Joel Goveya

Proofreader
Sandra Hopper

Indexer
Hemangini Bari

Graphics
Ronak Dhruv

Production Coordinator
Conidon Miranda

Cover Work
Conidon Miranda

About the Authors

Dr Xuewu Dai graduated (BEng) in Electronic Engineering and received his MSc in Computer Science, both from the Southwest University, Chongqing, China, in 1999 and 2003, respectively, and completed his PhD study at the School of Electrical and Electronic Engineering, University of Manchester, in 2008. He joined the School of Electronic and Information Engineering, Southwest University, as a Lecturer Assistant in 2002 and did research projects at University College London and University of Oxford.

As a researcher and R&D engineer in signal processing and dynamic system modeling, he has over 10 years' experience in MATLAB/Simulink simulation and embedded software development. More recently, he has been actively involved in wireless sensor actuator networks for various research and industrial projects (such as condition monitoring of aircraft engines, buildings, DFIG wind generators, CAN field-bus for SCADA, and optic sensors for water quality monitoring).

I would like to thank my wife Liping and my parents for their love, and allowing me to realize my own potential. I would like to thank Joel Goveya and Mohammed Fahad at Packt Publishing for their guidance throughout this process, and Amit Karpe and Ezequiel Aceto for their reviews. Finally, I would also like to acknowledge the partial financial support from the NSFC under grant 61101135.

Dr Fei Qin is currently an Assistant Professor in the Department of Electronic and Communications, University of Chinese Academy of Science, Beijing, China. He received his PhD degree from University College London, UK, in 2012. Prior to the start of his PhD, he was working for Crossbow Technology, Beijing Rep. Office as a Sr Application Engineer.

He has been working on the development of embedded systems for many different products and applications for almost ten years, including wireless network, sensor, and radar systems.

I would like to thank Dr Han, Zhengjun for his kindest advice on the motion detect algorithm, Joel Goveya and Mohammed Fahad at Packt Publishing for their support throughout this process, and Amit Karpe and Ezequiel Aceto for their reviews.

About the Reviewers

Ezequiel Aceto is a student at University of Buenos Aires (UBA), where he is attending Electronic Engineering and Computer Engineering. Also, he is a member of the Embedded Systems Labs at UBA.

He has more than eight years' experience of programming for mobile platforms like RIM's Blackberry, Google's Android, Apples iOS, and J2ME-enabled phones. Nowadays he works as CTO and Senior Developer at Everypost (`http://everypost.me`). Everypost is a mobile application that allows you to easily create multimedia content and post it simultaneously to your preferred social networks.

His first approach to embedded systems was at the age of 15 with the small BASIC Stamp I. And since then, he has worked with all kinds of microcontrollers (8-, 16-, and 32-bit) and programming languages, including BASIC, Assembly, C, C++, Java, Python, and Objective C.

He writes blog posts about embedded systems and mobile technologies at `www.ezequielaceto.com.ar`.

Amit Pandurang Karpe works for FireEye Inc., a global information security company, as a support engineer supporting their Asia-Pacific customers. He lives in Singapore with his wife, Swatee, and son, Sparsh. He has been active in the open source community from his college days, especially in Pune, where he was able to organize various activities with the help of vibrant and thriving communities such as PLUG, TechPune, ITMilan, Embedded Nirvana, and so on.

Currently he is working with the books "Getting Started with Cubieborad" and "Mastering Kali Linux for Advanced Penetration Testing".

I would like to thank the open source community without whom I couldn't have succeeded. A special thanks to the visionaries behind "BeagleBoard Project", who believed in open source hardware and led by example. Many thanks also to the community members, who keep doing a great job, which makes BeagleBoard a success.

I would like to thank the Packt Publication team, editors, project coordinator who keep doing the right things, so I can do my job to the best of my abilities.

I would like thank Pune Linux Users Group (PLUG), Embedded Group, and VSS friends, because of whom I am able to work on this project. I would also like to thank all my gurus, who helped me, and guided me in this field — Dr Vijay Gokhale, Sunil Dhadve, Sudhanwa Jogalekar, Bharathi Subramanian, Mohammed Khasim, and Niyam Bhushan.

Finally I would like to thank my family, my mother, my father, my brother, my son, and my wife, Swatee, without whose continuous support I could not have given my best efforts to this project.

www.PacktPub.com

Support files, eBooks, discount offers and more

You might want to visit www.PacktPub.com for support files and downloads related to your book.

Did you know that Packt offers eBook versions of every book published, with PDF and ePub files available? You can upgrade to the eBook version at www.PacktPub.com and as a print book customer, you are entitled to a discount on the eBook copy. Get in touch with us at service@packtpub.com for more details.

At www.PacktPub.com, you can also read a collection of free technical articles, sign up for a range of free newsletters and receive exclusive discounts and offers on Packt books and eBooks.

http://PacktLib.PacktPub.com

Do you need instant solutions to your IT questions? PacktLib is Packt's online digital book library. Here, you can access, read and search across Packt's entire library of books.

Why Subscribe?

- Fully searchable across every book published by Packt
- Copy and paste, print and bookmark content
- On demand and accessible via web browser

Free Access for Packt account holders

If you have an account with Packt at www.PacktPub.com, you can use this to access PacktLib today and view nine entirely free books. Simply use your login credentials for immediate access.

Table of Contents

Preface

The world of embedded system development has been evolving over the past few years with many emerging technologies in both the hardware and software fields. As an open source embedded single-board computer with many standard interfaces, BeagleBoard is an ideal embedded system development kit. Integrated with both an ARM 1GHz microprocessor and an IT's C6000 DSP processor, BeagleBoard's hardware is powerful enough to meet most demands of audio/video processing. The challenge now is how to design and implement a good digital processing algorithm on BeagleBoard quickly and easily, without intensive low-level coding. This book addresses this with the rapid prototyping tools of MATLAB/Simulink, including automatic embedded code generation and visual programming techniques, in a friendly Windows development environment.

This book is a hands-on guide for those interested in learning more about MATLAB/Simulink rapid prototyping techniques and practicing these techniques on a BeagleBoard.

Combing the power of BeagleBoard and MATLAB/Simulink, this book will walk you through a number of step-by-step exercises to give you a good grounding in rapid prototyping, and help you build your audio/video applications on a BeagleBoard. You can enjoy your ideas and algorithm development and let the big dog run your fancy inspiration.

What this book covers

Chapter 1, Introducing BeagleBoard, starts with an introduction to the BeagleBoard, followed by the concept of BeagleBoard-based rapid prototyping with MATLAB/Simulink. By the end of this chapter, the user will have a clear idea about the BeagleBoard and rapid prototyping on the Microsoft Windows platform.

Chapter 2, *Installing Linux on the BeagleBoard*, serves as a quick installation reference for new users and will look at setting up the BeagleBoard for rapid prototyping. We will then set up the development environment at a Windows 7 PC by installing some software and tools. Finally, we will connect the hardware and configure the BeagleBoard for rapid prototyping. By the end of this chapter, we will be ready to get started with our rapid prototyping and developing our applications.

Chapter 3, *C/C++ Development with Eclipse on Windows*, covers how to build our first program, a simple Hello World, at the Windows 7 host PC, and run it on the Linux BeagleBoard. We will be installing Eclipse Integrated Development Environment (IDE) and CodeBench Lite, a pure Windows-based cross-platform compiler on a Windows 7 host PC. Compared with setting up a cross-platform toolchain on a Linux host PC, the installation of a Windows-based toolchain is relatively straightforward, in which the configuration and path variable management are simplified with one click. Upon completion of this chapter, we will have a fully functional cross-development environment on Windows 7 and have a taste of the work flow of cross-platform embedded system development.

Chapter 4, *Automatic Code Generation*, looks at automatic code generation by MATLAB/ Simulink for rapid prototyping. In this chapter, instead of typing lines of C code manually, we will develop our applications either in high-level MATLAB scripts or in a Simulink graphical programming environment, and generate executable standalone applications for the BeagleBoard. Two projects will be demonstrated: a program for average operation and a music player, where the techniques of tuning parameters on the fly will be used for performance optimization.

Chapter 5, *Digital I/O and Serial Communication*, discusses how to utilize digital I/O and serial communication ports on the BeagleBoard to drive external sensors, for example, an IR sensor for motion detection in smart home applications. We will talk in detail about voltage shifting, digital I/O operation, serial communication, and the data processing of motion detection via an IR sensor.

Chapter 6, *Voice Recognition*, demonstrates the rapid prototyping of a voice recognition system on a BeagleBoard, including RMS voice detection, feature extraction, pattern matching, and decision making. The demo is designed to operate for single users, and may be used in multiuser applications. The program in the demo can be further extended for various applications, such as voice control and speaker authorization in smart home applications.

Chapter 7, Digital Video-Based Motion Detector, is a step-by-step tutorial on converting a low-cost USB web-camera and a BeagleBoard into a motion detector. We will move into the rapid prototyping of video processing and develop an algorithm for capturing video frames and tracking of a moving object in the sequence of video frames. With the video processing algorithm being validated, you will be able to easily integrate it into your own embedded system and build various advanced applications, such as home security, vision analysis, and traffic monitoring.

Appendix, Wrapping Up, reviews what we have learned and looks at other interesting projects and techniques that you may use to prototype your own BeagleBoard project. It also provides a collection of links pointing you towards the resources used in this book and other information and projects you may be interested in.

What you need for this book

Some basic skills in programming and experiences in MATLAB/Simulink are preferred. No prior knowledge of the Linux operating system or the BeagleBoard is needed, although exposure to these technologies will certainly be helpful. An in-depth knowledge of electronics is not required, and the book provides a step-by-step guide to setting up components and software in each chapter.

What you really need is a great idea about your applications and developing your algorithm in a user-friendly environment.

Who this book is for

This book is aimed towards the amateur embedded system enthusiasts, DIYs, students, academic researchers, and R&D engineers who have some basic skills in programming and are looking for a better solution to embedded software development to implement and validate their audio/video processing algorithms on hardware.

Conventions

In this book, you will find a number of styles of text that distinguish between different kinds of information. Here are some examples of these styles, and an explanation of their meaning.

Code words in text are shown as follows: "Here, nbFrame is the number of possible frames for an audio signal u with length lenSig."

A block of code is set as follows:

```
real_T calcavg(const real_T a[10])
{
  real_T y;
  int32_T k;
  /* UNTITLED2 Summary of this function goes here */
  /* Detailed explanation goes here */
  y = a[0];
  for (k = 0; k < 9; k++) {
    y += a[k + 1];
  }
  return y / 10.0;
}
```

Any command-line input or output is written as follows:

```
set_param(bdroot,'SimulationCommand','update');
```

New terms and **important words** are shown in bold. Words that you see on the screen, in menus or dialog boxes for example, appear in the text like this: "Click on the **Build** button to generate the C code."

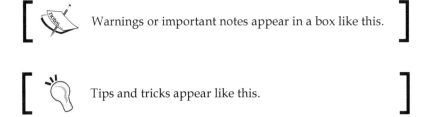

Warnings or important notes appear in a box like this.

Tips and tricks appear like this.

Reader feedback

Feedback from our readers is always welcome. Let us know what you think about this book—what you liked or may have disliked. Reader feedback is important for us to develop titles that you really get the most out of.

To send us general feedback, simply send an e-mail to feedback@packtpub.com, and mention the book title via the subject of your message.

If there is a topic that you have expertise in and you are interested in either writing or contributing to a book, see our author guide on www.packtpub.com/authors.

Customer support

Now that you are the proud owner of a Packt book, we have a number of things to help you to get the most from your purchase.

Downloading the example code

You can download the example code files for all Packt books you have purchased from your account at `http://www.packtpub.com`. If you purchased this book elsewhere, you can visit `http://www.packtpub.com/support` and register to have the files e-mailed directly to you.

Errata

Although we have taken every care to ensure the accuracy of our content, mistakes do happen. If you find a mistake in one of our books—maybe a mistake in the text or the code—we would be grateful if you would report this to us. By doing so, you can save other readers from frustration and help us improve subsequent versions of this book. If you find any errata, please report them by visiting `http://www.packtpub.com/submit-errata`, selecting your book, clicking on the **errata submission form** link, and entering the details of your errata. Once your errata are verified, your submission will be accepted and the errata will be uploaded on our website, or added to any list of existing errata, under the Errata section of that title. Any existing errata can be viewed by selecting your title from `http://www.packtpub.com/support`.

Piracy

Piracy of copyright material on the Internet is an ongoing problem across all media. At Packt, we take the protection of our copyright and licenses very seriously. If you come across any illegal copies of our works, in any form, on the Internet, please provide us with the location address or website name immediately so that we can pursue a remedy.

Please contact us at `copyright@packtpub.com` with a link to the suspected pirated material.

We appreciate your help in protecting our authors, and our ability to bring you valuable content.

Questions

You can contact us at `questions@packtpub.com` if you are having a problem with any aspect of the book, and we will do our best to address it.

1
Introducing BeagleBoard

This chapter provides an overview of this book and serves as an introduction to the BeagleBoard and rapid prototyping.

We'll first have a quick overview of what we will explore in this book, followed by a brief look at the features of BeagleBoard (with focus on the latest xM version) —an open source hardware platform borne for audio, video, and digital signal processing. Then we will introduce the concept of rapid prototyping and explain what we can do with the BeagleBoard support tools from MATLAB® and Simulink® by MathWorks®. Finally, this chapter ends with a summary.

Different from most approaches that involve coding and compiling at a Linux PC and require intensive manual configuration in command-line manner, the rapid prototyping approach presented in this book is a Windows-based approach that features a Windows PC for embedded software development through user-friendly graphic interaction and relieves the developer from intensive coding so that you can concentrate on your application and algorithms and have the BeagleBoard run your inspiration.

First of all, let's begin with a quick overview of this book.

A quick overview of this book

In this book, we will go through a number of exciting projects to demonstrate how to build a prototype of an embedded audio, video, and digital signal processing system rapidly without intensive programming and coding. The main contents of this book and projects include:

- Install Linux for BeagleBoard from a Windows PC
- Developing C/C++ with Eclipse on a Windows PC

- Automatic embedded code generation for BeagleBoard

- Serial communication and digital I/O application: Infrared motion detector

- Audio application: voice recognition

- Video application: motion detection

By completing each chapter in the book, you will understand the workflow of building an embedded system. You will learn about setting up the development environment, writing software at a host PC running Microsoft Windows, and compiling the code for standalone ARM-executables at the BeagleBoard running Linux. Then you will learn the skills of rapid prototyping embedded audio and video systems via the BeagleBoard support tools from Simulink by MathWorks.

The main features of the techniques presented in this book are

- Open source hardware

- A Windows-based friendly development environment

- Rapid prototyping and easy learning without intensive coding

These features will save you from intensive coding and will also relieve the pressure on you to build an embedded audio/video processing system without learning the complicated embedded Linux. The rapid prototyping techniques presented allow you to concentrate on your brilliant concept and algorithm design, rather than being distracted by the complicated embedded system and low-level manual programming. This is beneficial for students and academics who are primarily interested in the development of audio/video processing algorithms, and want to build an embedded prototype for proof-of-concept quickly.

BeagleBoard-xM

BeagleBoard, the brainchild of a small group of **Texas Instruments** (TI) engineers and volunteers, is a pocket-sized, low-cost, fan-less, single-board computer containing TI **Open Multimedia Application Platform 3** (**OMAP3**) **System on a chip** (**SoC**) processor, which integrates a 1 GHz ARM core and a TI's **Digital Signal Processor** (**DSP**) together. Since many consumer electronics devices nowadays run some form of embedded Linux-based environment and usually are on an ARM-based platform, the BeagleBoard was proposed as an inexpensive development kit for hobbyists, academics, and professionals for high-performance, ARM-based embedded system learning and evaluation. As an open hardware embedded computer with open source software development in mind, the BeagleBoard was created for audio, video, and digital signal processing with the purpose of meeting the demands of those who want to get involved with embedded system development and build their own embedded devices or solutions.

Furthermore, by utilizing standard interfaces, the BeagleBoard comes with all of the expandability of today's desktop machines. The developers can easily bring their own peripherals and turn the pocket-sized BeagleBoard into a single-board computer with many additional features.

The following figure shows the PCB layout and major components of the latest xM version of the BeagleBoard. The BeagleBoard-xM (referred to as BeagleBoard in this book unless specified otherwise) is an 8.25 x 8.25cm (3.25" x 3.25") circuit board that includes the following components:

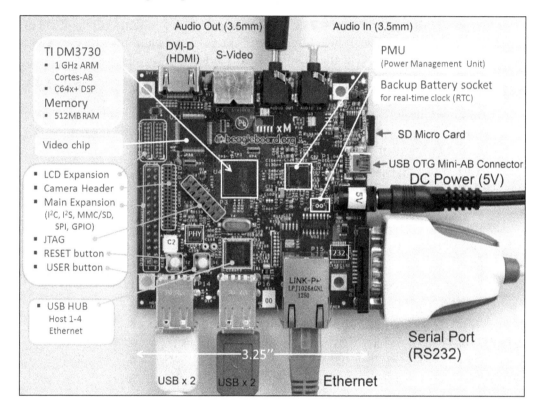

- **CPU**: TI's DM3730 processor, which houses a 1 GHz ARM Cortex-A8 superscalar core and a TI's C64x+ DSP core. The power of the 32-bit ARM and C64+ DSP, plus a large amount of onboard DDR RAM arm the BeagleBoard with the capacity to deal with computational intensive tasks, such as audio and video processing.

- **Memory**: 512 MB MDDR SDRAM working 166MHz. The processor and the 512 MB RAM comes in a .44 mm (Package on Package) POP package, where the memory is mounted on top of the processor.

- **microSD card slot**: being provided as a means for the main nonvolatile memory. The SD cards are where we install our operating system and will act as a hard disk. The BeagleBoard is shipped with a 4GB microSD card containing factory-validated software (actually, an Angstrom distribution of embedded Linux tailored for BeagleBoard). Of course, this storage can be easily expanded by using, for example, an USB portable hard drive.

- **USB2.0 On-The-Go (OTG) mini port**: This port can be used as a communication link to a host PC and the power source deriving power from the PC over the USB cable.

- **4-port USB-2.0 hub**: These four USB Type A connectors with full LS/FS/HS support. Each port can provide power `on`/`off` control and up to 500 mA as long as the input DC to the BeagleBoard is at least 3 A.

- **RS232 port**: A single RS232 port via UART3 of DM3730 processor is provided by a DB9 connector on BeagleBoard-xM. A USB-to-serial cable can be plugged directly into the DB9 connector. By default, when the BeagleBoard boots, system information will be sent to the RS232 port and you can log in to the BeagleBoard through it.

- **10/100 M Ethernet**: The Ethernet port features auto-MDIX, which works for both crossover cable and straight-through cable.

- **Stereo audio output and input**: BeagleBoard has a hardware accelerated audio encoding and decoding (CODEC) chip and provides stereo in and out ports via two 3.5 mm jacks to support external audio devices, such as headphones, powered speakers, and microphones (either stereo or mono).

- **Video interfaces**: It includes S-video and **Digital Visual Interface** (**DVI**)-D output, LCD port, a Camera port.

- **Joint Test Action Group (JTAG) connector**: reset button, a user button, and many developer-friendly expansion connectors. The user button can be used as an application button.

To get going, we need to power the BeagleBoard by either the USB OTG mini port, which just provides current of up to 500 mA to run the board alone, or a 5V power source to run with external peripherals. The BeagleBoard boots from the microSD card once the power is on. Various alternative software images are available on the BeagleBoard website, so we can replace the factory default images and have the BeagleBoard run with many other popular embedded operating systems (like Andria and Windows CE). The **off-the-shelf expansion** via standard interfaces on the BeagleBoard allows developers to choose various components and operating systems they prefer to build their own embedded solutions or a desktop-like system as shown below:

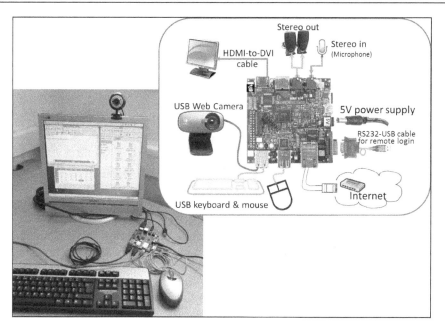

BeagleBoard for rapid prototyping

A rapid prototyping approach allows you to quickly create a working implementation of your proof-of-concept and verify your audio or video applications on hardware early, which overcomes barriers in the design-implementation-validation loops and helps you find the right solution for your applications. Rapid prototyping not only reduces the development time from concept to product, but also allows you to identify defects and mistakes in system and algorithm design at an early stage. Prototyping your concept and evaluating its performance on a target hardware platform gives you confidence in your design, and promotes its success in applications.

The powerful BeagleBoard equipped with many standard interfaces provides a good hardware platform for rapid embedded system prototyping. On the other hand, the rapid prototyping tool, the **BeagleBoard Support from Simulink** package, provided by MathWorks with **graphic user interface (GUI)** allows developers to easily implement their concept and algorithm graphically in Simulink, and then directly run the algorithms at the BeagleBoard. In short, *you design algorithms in MATLAB/ Simulink and see them perform as a standalone application on the BeagleBoard*. In this way, you can concentrate on your brilliant concept and algorithm design, rather than being distracted by the complicated embedded system and low-level manual programming.

The prototyping tool reduces the steep learning curve of embedded systems and helps hobbyists, students, and academics who have a great idea, but have little background knowledge of embedded systems. This feature is particularly useful to those who want to build a prototype of their applications in a short time.

MathWorks introduced the BeagleBoard support package for rapid prototyping in 2010. Since the release of MATLAB 2012a, support for the BeagleBoard-xM has been integrated into Simulink and is also available in the student version of MATLAB and Simulink. Your rapid prototyping starts with modeling your systems and implementing algorithms in MATLAB and Simulink. From your models, you can automatically generate algorithmic C code along with processor-specific, real-time scheduling code and peripheral drivers, and run them as standalone executables on embedded processors in real time. The following steps provide an overview of the work flow for BeagleBoard rapid prototyping in MATLAB/Simulink:

1. Create algorithms for various applications in Simulink and MATLAB with a user-friendly GUI. The applications can be audio processing (for example, digital amplifiers), computer vision applications (for example, object tracking), control systems (for example, flight control), and so on.

2. Verify and improve the algorithm work by simulation. With intensive simulation, it is expected that most defects, errors, and mistakes in algorithms will be identified. Then the algorithms are easily modified and updated to fix the identified issues.

3. Run the algorithms as standalone applications on the BeagleBoard.

4. Interactive parameter turning, signal monitoring, and performance optimization of applications running on the BeagleBoard.

Summary

In this chapter, we have familiarized ourselves with the BeagleBoard and rapid prototyping by using MATLAB/Simulink. We have also looked at the features of the rapid prototyping we are going to explore in this book and the basic steps in rapid prototyping in MATLAB/Simulink.

With this in mind, we will get started on our first project— setting up the BeagleBoard-xM.

2
Installing Linux on the BeagleBoard

In order to use the BeagleBoard, we will need to connect it with peripheral hardware and install an operating system. This chapter will look at setting up the BeagleBoard for rapid prototyping. We will start by setting up the BeagleBoard hardware. We then install some software and tools on a Windows 7 PC, on which we will install an embedded Linux operating system onto an SD card. Once this is done, you insert the SD card into the BeagleBoard's SD card slot and power on. Then you will have a BeagleBoard running Linux and working like a desktop PC.

This chapter will cover the following topics in a step-by-step manner:

- Setting up and connecting hardware
- Installing software and tools on a Windows 7 PC
- Installing the precompiled Ubuntu operating system on the Windows 7 PC
- Configuring the BeagleBoard

By the end of this chapter, we will be ready to get started with our rapid prototyping and developing our applications.

Let's start by setting up the hardware for rapid prototyping.

Setting up the hardware

Since the BeagleBoard comes with no cables or connectors, this section will discuss the required and optional additional hardware for BeagleBoard development and illustrate how to connect these peripheral devices to have a working BeagleBoard.

Like working with other embedded devices, developing with BeagleBoard generally involves the use of two systems, a desktop development system and the BeagleBoard itself. For convenience, the BeagleBoard hardware is occasionally referred to as "target hardware" or "target system" and the desktop system is referred to as "host computer" or "host PC". In this book, the host computer we are using is a common desktop PC running Windows 7.

Compulsory hardware

You need several cables and accessories for setting up a minimum BeagleBoard development environment. They are as follows:

- A host computer that can be a desktop or laptop computer with USB, Ethernet ports, and SD card reader. We need the SD card reader to prepare the BeagleBoard's operating system, since BeagleBoard uses a SD card as its hard drive.

- Power supply that can be a USB-A to Mini-B cable or a separate 5V wall-adapter power supply. Power via the USB OTG port may work, but it is not recommended, as the BeagleBoard attempts to draw more than 500mA of current and, the current supply by a USB port is limited to 500mA in most cases. It is better to have a 5V, at least 1A, wall-adapter power supply, with a 5.5 x 2.1 mm barrel type, tip positive, grounded outer barrel connector.

- A RS232 to USB adapter cable for serial communication between the BeagleBoard and the host computer. If you have a serial COM port on the host computer, you may use a DB9 null modem serial cable.

- An Ethernet cable for communication and login.

- An Ethernet hub with Internet access. We will have the BeagleBoard and the windows PC connected to the hub, so that the BeagleBoard can access the Internet and the PC can access the BeagleBoard via Ethernet connections.

Required hardware for rapid prototyping in this book

In this chapter, we only need the necessary hardware to set up a minimum BeagleBoard development system. As we go further in rapid prototyping for motion detection, audio, and video applications, we may need more peripheral devices to interact with the physical world and users. In succeeding chapters, we will need the following devices:

- A monitor with DVI-D input interface. An LCD monitor is recommended.
- An HDMI to DVI-D cable.
- Stereo speakers or earphones with 3.5mm jack.
- A microphone with 3.5mm jack.
- A Logitech HD Webcam C310 with a USB interface.
- An ePIR (passive infrared) motion-detecting sensor by Zilog.
- A Trainer-xM Board by Tincan for I/O expansion and breakout.

  This breakout board extends the serial port, SPI, and I2C interfaces of BeagleBoard's main expansion header with level shift (+3.3V).

The ePIR sensor by Zilog and the Trainer-xM Board will be used in *Chapter 5, Digital I/O and Serial Communication*, where you will find more details of these two devices.

Connecting our components

When you have the peripheral devices, it is time to start plugging things in. Connecting the devices is a fairly easy task, as both the BeagleBoard and these devices have a standard interface for connection. Here, we only connect the BeagleBoard with these compulsory components to set up a minimum development system, install support tools at the Windows 7 host PC, and set up the Linux operating system at the BeagleBoard.

Follow these steps in order to connect up these compulsory components:

1. Connect the RS232-to-USB cable's DB9-end into the BeagleBoard's serial port. Its USB-end goes to a spare USB port on the host PC.
2. Connect the Ethernet cable to the BeagleBoard and to the hub.
3. Connect speakers or headphones.
4. If you have not connected the host computer to the hub, connect it now.

Please note that we have not connected the power cable yet. Powering the BeagleBoard is the last step after we have all the software and firmware in place.

Installing software and tools on a Windows 7 PC

The BeagleBoard is fast by embedded standards and it will give your embedded system a run for its money, but it is not designed for some complicated tasks, such as compiling piles of source code to get an executable Linux kernel. Therefore, the widely-accepted practice for embedded system development is to develop and build software on a powerful desktop PC system (host PC) and then transfer the resulting executable software to the target system (which is the BeagleBoard in this book).

Target and host PC systems

Compared to the target embedded system, the host PC usually has a much more powerful CPU and huge memory. In theory, you can write your code and compile them at your target hardware, the BeagleBoard. This approach is called **native complier**, as you have a compiler installed at the BeagleBoard to build your software. However, compiling is time and resource consuming, especially when you are developing large software. It is not a reasonable task for embedded systems, which will take much longer than compiling at a PC.

In practice, we usually have a host PC working as a software development machine for coding, compiling, and debugging. This approach is called **cross-compiler**, as the host PC usually has different hardware and software infrastructure. It does not matter whether the host PC platform runs Linux, Windows, or Mac, as long as it can communicate with the BeagleBoard over a serial port and/or Ethernet.

In this book, we are using a common laptop running Windows 7 operating system on our host PC. This section shows how to install support software and tools for BeagleBoard hardware at the Windows 7 host PC.

Finding the COM port for a RS232-USB adapter cable

As mentioned in step 1 of connecting the RS232-to-USB cable to a spare USB port on the host PC, you usually will get a **Found New Hardware Wizard** window on your Windows 7 PC.

You may get the following message:

Your device is ready to use

Device driver software installed successfully.

If you see the preceding message, please go to step 3 of finding COM port in Windows **Device Manager** as explained in the following steps.

If the error message **Device driver software was not successfully installed** pops up, the RS232-USB cable is not recognized correctly and will be identified as an **Unknown Device**. Simply close the pop-up window and follow these steps:

1. Download the driver for your RS232-to-USB adapter cable. If it is necessary, please contact the manufacturer to download the driver.

2. Go to the Windows device manager by navigating to **Start** | **Control Panel** | **Device Manager**, and navigate the device tree to find the **Unknown Device**. Right-click on the **Unknown Device** and click on **Update Driver Software**. And follow the instructions therein to finish the driver installation.

3. Navigate to **Start** | **Control Panel** | **Device Manager**, then navigate the device tree, expand the item **Ports (COM & LPT)** and check if a COM port has been created successfully, as shown in the following screenshot.

Write down the port number. For example, the port number is **4** in the following following screenshot:

 If you have more than one COM port listed in your device manager, disconnect and reconnect the RS232-USB cable; the COM port that disappears and then shows up again is the correct port for BeagleBoard communication. In some cases, the USB serial port adapters do not appear immediately after you install the driver. To solve this issue, simply disconnect and reconnect the cable, or reboot your host PC.

Configuring the IP address of the host PC

Once we have connected the BeagleBoard to the host PC either directly through an Ethernet cable or through an Ethernet hub, we need to set up correct IP configurations at both the host PC and the BeagleBoard sides. In this section, we will look at the IP configuration at the host PC side. The IP configuration at the BeagleBoard side will be examined in the section *Installing Ubuntu for BeagleBoard on a Windows 7 PC*.

Provided the BeagleBoard and host PC are connected via an Ethernet hub with DHCP services, it is recommended to have your host PC obtain an IP address from the DHCP server. DHCP is a network service that automatically configures the IP settings for Ethernet devices. Follow the given steps to let your host PC obtain the IP address automatically:

1. Open the control panel of Windows 7, choose **Network and Internet**, and then click on **Network and Sharing Center**. Then on the left panel, select **Change adapter settings** to list the network adapters of your host PC, as shown in the following screenshot:

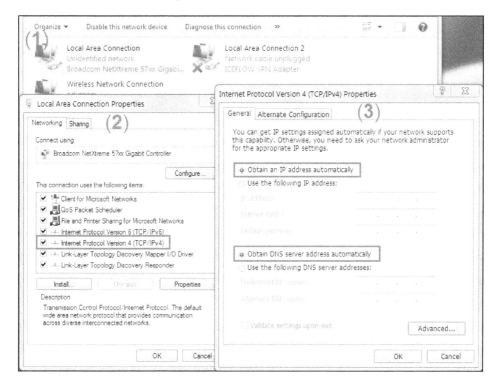

2. Find the **Local Area Connection** that is used for your BeagleBoard and double click on it to open the **Local Area Connection Properties** dialog.

3. Double click on **Internet Protocol Version 4 (TCP/IPv4)** in the item box of the dialog window to open the **Internet Protocol Version 4 (TCP/IPv4) Properties** window.

4. In the **Internet Protocol Version 4 (TCP/IPv4) Properties** window, select **Obtain an IP address automatically** radio button and select **Obtain DNS server address automatically** (as shown in previous screenshot).

5. Click on the **OK** buttons of these windows to finish the IP configuration.

Manually assign IP addresses

If the BeagleBoard is directly connected to an Ethernet port on the host PC, you need to assign static IP addresses to both the host PC and the BeagleBoard. To do so, in the previous step 4, you need to select **Use the following IP address** radio button and manually set the IP address. For example, you may use the following configuration for the host PC, enter **IP address** as 192.168.2.1, **Subnet mask** as 255.255.255.0, and **Default gateway** as 192.168.2.1. Please also note that, in static IP assignment, we also need to manually set the BeagleBoard with an IP address in the same network segment as the host PC. For example, enter **IP address** as 192.168.2.2 and **Subnet mask** as 255.255.255.0 for the BeagleBoard.

Installing MATLAB and the BeagleBoard support package

For rapid prototyping a BeagleBoard embedded audio/video processing system, we are making use of the BeagleBoard hardware support package and automatic code generation provided by MATLAB and Simulink. We will look at how to install MATLAB/Simulink with the BeagleBoard support package.

What are MATLAB and Simulink

MATLAB and Simulink are computing and simulation tools developed by MathWorks, the world's leading developer of technical computing software for engineers, scientists, and economists in industry and education. MATLAB (**mat**rix **lab**oratory) is a numerical computing environment that allows matrix manipulations, data plotting, implementation of data processing algorithms, and interfacing with programs written in other languages, including C, C++, Java, and Fortran. Simulink is a graphical programming tool for modeling, simulating, and analyzing dynamic systems. The graphical block diagramming interface in Simulink allows you to develop your computing algorithms by dragging-and-dropping blocks and connecting blocks by signal wires.

Why we use MATLAB/Simulink for rapid prototyping

The attracting features of using MATLAB/Simulink for BeagleBoard software development are the automatic code generation and the performance optimization by tuning parameters on the fly. This is a fast and inexpensive way for hobbyists and engineers to verify and evaluate their designs early, so that design defects can be found and fixed early.

You can design your data processing algorithms in a user-friendly graphical modular environment and then, in a few minutes time and without intensive manual coding, you see your algorithms running as standalone applications on the BeagleBoard. This is particularly useful when your application involves complicated audio/video processing and needs many trial-and-error iterations for performance optimization.

The advantages of rapid prototyping by MATLAB/Simulink are as follows:

- Focus on innovation and data processing algorithm design.
- Allows you to work in design, coding, deployment, and testing and move quickly between each process.

 You can perform design-testing iterations in minutes rather than weeks.

- Simulink models and data processing algorithms can be auto-coded to C, compiled, and deployed as standalone applications at BeagleBoard.
- Graphical modular programming and automatic code generation make embedded software development easier.
- Obvious advantages for small research project and student DIYs in terms of shorter development time and easier learning curves.
- Intensive simulation to enable "right-first-time" design.

And most importantly, the BeagleBoard support from MATLAB/Simulink now has wide availability and easy access for free. Since MATLAB 2012a, Simulink has a built-in support for BeagleBoard. This BeagleBoard support is also available in MATLAB and Simulink Student Version. You may also ask MathWorks for a trial version (`https://www.mathworks.co.uk/products/matlab/trial.html`) which also includes the built-in BeagleBoard support.

Installing MATLAB

Suppose you have got a Student Version of MATLAB and Simulink (2013a) and want to install it on your Windows 7 computer. A typical installation requires around 4GB disk and at least 1GB RAM. Follow these steps to install MATLAB:

1. Before you begin, make sure your computer is connected to the Internet and you have administrator privileges to install the software. You may register for a free MathWorks account by clicking on **Create Account** on the webpage www.mathworks.com. Alternatively, you can create one during the installation process.

2. If you have the installation DVD, insert the DVD; it will automatically start the installation. If you download the installation files at your local hard drive, or the DVD installation does not start automatically, double-click on the installer setup.exe in the DVD or the folder where you saved your downloaded installation files.

3. Following the instructions of the installer to complete the installation. During the installation, the **Product Selection** dialog will ask you to select the products you want to install and you should have MATLAB, Simulink, MATLAB Coder, and Embedded Coder selected.

4. At the end of installation, you will be asked for activation. Follow the instructions therein to activate it. You will need your e-mail address, MathWorks account information, and the digital image of the proof of your student status.

More details and a step-by-step tutorial of installing and activating a Student Version of MATLAB and Simulink can be found at http://www.mathworks.com/help/install/sv/installing-and-activating-student-version.html.

Installing the built-in BeagleBoard support package

Once you have MATLAB installed and activated on your Windows 7 host PC, run the MATLAB program as administrator and type targetinstaller in the MATLAB command window followed by pressing the *Enter* key. This starts the BeagleBoard Support Package Installer. Simply follow the instructions and default settings provided by the Support Package Installer to complete the installation.

This process downloads and installs a Simulink block library called Simulink Support Package for BeagleBoard Hardware, demo examples, and some third-party tools (such as SDL, Wget for Windows and 7-zip) on your host computer.

Installing Ubuntu for BeagleBoard on a Windows 7 PC

After installing the development software on the host PC, we now need to install an embedded operating system to a microSD card for BeagleBoard. We will install a precompiled image (that contains the Ubuntu operating system for BeagleBoard) into the microSD card. Using a precompiled image is much easier and faster than building your own operating system. An automated installation tool called **targetupdater** has been provided in MATLAB for automated installation and configuration.

Follow the succeeding steps to install the Linux operating system (Ubuntu 11.04) for BeagleBoard. A detailed step-by-step guide can be found at www.mathworks.com/ help/simulink/ug/update-firmware-on-the-beagleboard-hardware.html.

1. Start the update firmware process using one of the following methods:

    ° Click on **Continue** at the end of the targetinstaller process

    ° Or enter targetupdater in the MATLAB command window

2. In the **Update firmware** dialog, choose **BeagleBoard** and click on **Next**.

3. Choose your board version (that is, **BeagleBoard-xM**) and click on **Next**.

4. Connect the BeagleBoard as we described earlier (also as shown in the update firmware window) and click on **Next**.

5. Choose to get the firmware image from the Internet or from a folder. The default option is Internet. The file size of the firmware image is approximately 1GB. Downloading the firmware can take from 2 to 60 minutes, or more.

Image file

The image file you downloaded is an Ubuntu 11.04 operating system tailored for BeagleBoard-xM and is usually named with a filename beginning with beagleboard_ubuntu. For example, beagleboard_ubuntu_11_04_r4_12_08_2011.img.7z in your download folder. For experienced users, you can unzip this file into a *.img file and use image writing tools (such as **Win32 Disk Imager** for Windows) to write the image file into a microSD card manually.

6. When the downloading process completes, you will be asked to insert a 4 GB microSD card into the host PC. The microSD card will be recognized as a driver (a removable storage device) in Windows 7. Then you need to select the correct driver letter for the microSD card.

7. Click on **Write**. This process takes several minutes to complete.

[
It is critical to select the right driver for the microSD card. As the update firmware tool will format and overwrite the driver you select with the Ubuntu firmware, if you unfortunately select an incorrect driver letter (for example, your hard drive) by mistake, your hard drive will be formatted.
]

Once it completes, eject the microSD card from the card reader at the host PC and insert it into the BeagleBoard's microSD card slot.

Now we have completed the embedded operating system installation for BeagleBoard. We will continue to configure the BeagleBoard for rapid prototyping.

Configuring BeagleBoard

In this section, we will set up the serial and Ethernet connections by continuing the targetupdater process provided by MATLAB and Simulink. Follow these steps to do it:

1. Go back to the targetupdater dialog and select the COM port of the RS232-USB connection to the BeagleBoard. As we discussed earlier, the COM port for the BeagleBoard can be found from Windows **Device Manager**.

2. Power on the BeagleBoard by the 5V wall adapter and press the **RESET** button of the BeagleBoard to reboot. Then click on **Next** in the targetupdater dialog. When a reset of BeagleBoard is detected, it displays the progress of the booting of the BeagleBoard.

3. Configure the IP address of the BeagleBoard. After the BeagleBoard is booted up, you will have a configure board dialog (see the following screenshot). Type in a unique name for the BeagleBoard (for example, myBBxM-01). Supposing you connect the BeagleBoard and host PC via the Ethernet hub with DHCP services, it is recommended to use dynamic IP address configuration for the BeagleBoard. Here, we select **Automatically get IP address** and leave the other input boxes as they are. Then click on **Configure**.

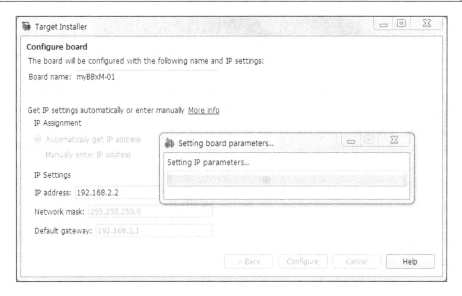

4. The targetupdater will set up a serial connection and applies the settings to the BeagleBoard. If you succeed, you will have a confirmation window with the board information (board name, IP address, account name, and password). Make a note of the board information, which will be used for remote login to the BeagleBoard. Click on **Next** and then on **Finish** to complete the configuration of the BeagleBoard.

Before the installer exits, you will select if you want to open demos after installation. If you wish, you can check the **Launch target demos** checkbox and the demo page for BeagleBoard will open. You can select the demo to explore the features of BeagleBoard support packages.

First interaction with the BeagleBoard

You have now successfully completed the BeagleBoard setup and will see the LEDs at the BeagleBoard flash. One optional final test you can perform is to connect to your BeagleBoard from your Windows host PC via Ethernet and/or the serial-USB connection.

Installing PuTTY on a Windows PC

We will use a terminal to connect to the BeagleBoard. For Windows systems, the most popular terminal program is PuTTY, which provides a terminal-style window to connect to Linux systems. The PuTTY installer (a single executable file) can be downloaded from `tartarus.org/~simon/putty-snapshots/x86/putty-installer.exe` and more information about PuTTY can be found at `www.chiark.greenend.org.uk/~sgtatham/putty/download.html`.

 Terminal in the early days was a hardware device used for entering data into, and displaying data from, a Unix-like computer machine. Nowadays, terminal (or terminal emulator) is referred to as a software program with a command-line interface, which simulates the functionality of a hardware terminal and allows the user to interact with the Unix/Linux computer in a text-based manner. Typical terminal programs include Terminal. app for OS X and PuTTY for Windows.

Download the installer (for example, `putty-0.62-installer.exe`) to your host PC, double-click on the installer file and follow the wizard therein to install PuTTY.

Logging into BeagleBoard from a Windows PC

When installation completes, you will see a new program group named PuTTY. Click on the PuTTY icon to launch the terminal.

When PuTTY starts, the configuration page will first display (as shown in the following screenshot). In the **Host Name (or IP address)** input box, type the IP address of your BeagleBoard. In the **Port** input box, enter 22 and, under **Connection type**, select **SSH**. Finally, click on the **Open** button.

 Since the IP address of your BeagleBoard may change in the future, or you may forget your BeagleBoard's IP address, you can press the **USER** button of BeagleBoard to hear the BeagleBoard speak its IP address at any time.

The following screenshot shows the **PuTTY Configuration** window for remote login:

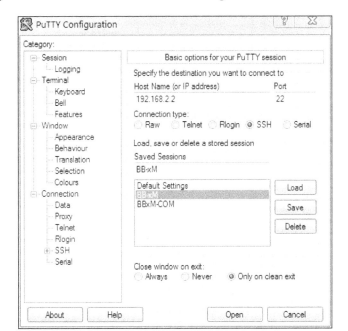

You may see a pop-up window titled **PuTTY Security Alert** and a message explaining that the server's host key is not cached in the registry. Click on the **Yes** button to continue and a terminal window with a command-line interface opens.

In the terminal window, you will now see a prompt **Login as**. If the **Login as** prompt is not displayed, press *Enter* once and you will see it. Now we follow these steps to log in to the BeagleBoard:

1. Enter the username, which is `ubuntu` by default, and press *Enter*.

2. When you are asked for password, enter the default password `temppwd` and press *Enter*.

3. You will now be logged into the BeagleBoard and you should see the command prompt.

You have now successfully tested the SSH server and, if you wish, can now control your BeagleBoard remotely from your Windows PC. One thing you would like to try is to find the IP address of your BeagleBoard from the command line. Enter the `ifconfig` command at the terminal window; you will get something like the following:

ubuntu@myBBxM-01:~$ ifconfig

eth0   Link encap:Ethernet HWaddr 22:20:32:0a:28:f3

>   **inet addr:192.168.2.2 Bcast:192.168.2.255 Mask:255.255.255.0**

>   **inet6 addr: fe80::2020:32ff:fe0a:28f3/64 Scope:Link**

>   **UP BROADCAST RUNNING MULTICAST MTU:1488 Metric:1**

It tells you the the IP address of your BeagleBoard is **192.168.2.2** with network mask **255.255.255.0**.

Logging in via a serial-USB connection

Alternatively, you can log into your BeagleBoard via the serial-USB connection as well. You need to first find which COM port (for example COM4) of your host PC is used for the serial-USB connection; see the preceding section *Finding the COM port for a RS232-USB adapter cable*.

Launch a PuTTY terminal and, at the configuration page of PuTTY, click on **Session** on the left panel. At the main configuration panel, select the **Serial** radio button under **Connection type**. Enter the COM port (for example COM4) in the **Serial line** field and `115200` in the **Speed** field.

You may need to configure the parameters of serial connection. On the left panel, select **Serial** under **Connection** and set the parameters (see the following screenshot) **Speed (baud)** as 115200, **Data bits** as 8, **Stop bits** as 1, **Parity** to **None**, and **Flow control** to **None**.

Using Win32 Disk Imager to create multiple microSD cards

In some cases, you may want to create several microSD cards for your BeagleBoards, for example, if you have several BeagleBoards. You can repeat the MATLAB targetupdater procedure. Since you have downloaded the image file of the Linux operating system (Ubuntu 11.04), an alternative and quick way is the Win32 Disk Imager utility, which is an open source program for Windows to write images to or create images from SD cards.

Follow these steps to create your microSD card manually:

1. Download Win32 Disk Imager (a zip file) at sourceforge.net/projects/win32diskimager/.

2. Unzip the file to a local folder and run the executable file Win32DiskImager.exe in the unzipped folder.

3. In the **Win32 Disk Imager** window, browse to the image file (usually a *.img file) that contains the operation system for the BeagleBoard. Select the right letter for your SD card (e.g. **N:** in the following figure).

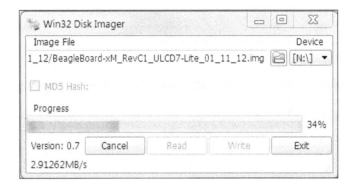

4. Clicking on the **Write** button will write the image file to the SD card.

Summary

In this chapter, we have familiarized ourselves with the additional hardware devices and understood what the host computer is. We have looked at how we connect these devices, set up the Windows PC as a host computer, and install the Linux operating system for the BeagleBoard from the Windows host PC. Finally, we have learned about using the PuTTY terminal program to log into the BeagleBoard and control it.

There are many resources available online if you wish to further explore the BeagleBoard, the Ubuntu operating system, and the MATLAB/Simulink support package for BeagleBoard. These include the following:

- BeagleBoard-xM Community: http://beagleboard.org/Products/BeagleBoard-xM
- Ubuntu at BeagleBoard: http://elinux.org/BeagleBoardUbuntu
- BeagleBoard Support from MATLAB/Simulink: www.mathworks.co.uk/hardware-support/beagleboard.html
- Ubuntu community and support documents: https://help.ubuntu.com/community

Now we have the rapid prototyping tools at the host PC in place and get the BeagleBoard setup ready to run the software we are going to develop. We can now move onto our first project—developing a Hello World! program at your host Windows PC and running it on your BeagleBoard.

3
C/C++ Development with Eclipse on Windows

So far we have set up our BeagleBoard and have been able to log in to it from the Windows 7 host PC. Now we can start building programs and applications using the BeagleBoard. Generally, we have two basic approaches for rapid prototyping:

- **Textual programming using MATLAB**: We develop our source code in MATLAB, generate C/C++ code, and compile them into the BeagleBoard-compatible executables. MATLAB does not provide the cross-compiler for BeagleBoard, so we need to manually set up an external cross-compiler (in this book, the Eclipse IDE and Sourcery CodeBench compiler).

- **Graphical programming in Simulink**: In this approach, we develop our program graphically in Simulink. The generated C/C++ code from Simulink are downloaded to and compiled natively on the BeagleBoard. Thus there is no need for an additional cross-compiler. Only the MATLAB/Simulink development environment is required.

If you are going for the graphical programming approach only, you can skip this chapter and jump to *Chapter 4*, *Automatic Code Generation*, section *Simulink Code Generation*.

In this chapter, we are going to build our first program, a simple Hello World!, at the Windows 7 host PC, and run it on the Linux BeagleBoard. We will be installing Eclipse — the most popular open source and graphical **Integrated Development Environment (IDE)**, and **Sourcery CodeBench Lite**, a free open source Windows-based cross-platform compiler, on the host PC. Then we will use the Eclipse IDE and cross-compiler to compile C/C++ source code, and get the executable program that will run on the BeagleBoard. Compared with setting up a cross-platform toolchain on a Linux host PC, the installation of a Windows-based toolchain is relatively straightforward, in which the configuration and path variable management are simplified with one click.

There are several steps needed to get you up and running your first `Hello World!` project:

- Installing CodeBench Lite, a pure Windows-based cross-complier
- Installing Eclipse IDE and toolkits on the Windows 7 host PC
- Creating your first cross-platform project—`Hello World!`

Upon completion of this chapter, you will have a fully functional cross-development environment on Windows 7, and have a taste of the workflow of cross-platform embedded system development.

Windows-based cross-compiler

Now we have the hardware for our rapid prototyping, we will need to develop software to make use of the capabilities of the hardware. Since compiling on a desktop PC is much faster than compiling on an embedded system, as a common approach in practice, we are editing, compiling, and building code on a Windows host PC to get ARM-compatible programs that will be running on the Linux BeagleBoard. The distinguishing feature of this approach is the cross-platform development: the executable program is built on an x86-Windows platform, but runs on a different ARM-Linux embedded system. In order to do this, you need a cross-platform toolchain with a cross-compiler for your BeagleBoard.

 A **cross-compiler** is able to create an executable program for a platform other than the one on which the compiler is running. In our scenario, the compiler runs on a Windows machine (usually with an x86 processor), but its outputs are executables for an ARM processor. A **toolchain** is a set of distinct software development tools that are linked (or chained) together by specific stages. Usually, a toolchain contains text editors, compilers, and debuggers.

Installing Sourcery CodeBench Lite in Windows

CodeBench Lite is a free cross-compiler and toolchain created by CodeSourcery (now acquired by Mentor Graphics) for ARM processors in cooperation with ARM Ltd. CodeBench Lite includes C/C++ compilers, assemblers, linkers, and libraries for building an ARM-compatible executable program. It supports Windows XP/7 systems (including both 32-bit and 64-bit versions). The Windows-version CodeBench Lite features a graphical installer that manages the path variables and simplifies the configuration.

Follow these steps to download and install CodeBench Lite:

1. Download CodeBench Lite from `http://www.mentor.com/embedded-software/sourcery-tools/sourcery-codebench/editions/lite-edition/`. There are many supported processors on that page. Please scroll down to the **ARM Processors** section and select the **GNU/Linux release**, and then select the **IA32 Windows Installer**. The Windows-version installer is provided as an executable file with the `.exe` extension (for example, `arm-2013.05-24-arm-none-linux-gnueabi.exe`, which is about 151MB). You may need to first register with your e-mail to get the download link.

2. Double-click on the executable file that you just downloaded, to start the installation. The graphical installer will guide you through the process.

3. When the installer asks **Choose Install Folder**, it is recommended to use a simple path like `C:\CodeSourcery` rather than the default one `C:\Program Files\CodeSourcery\Sourcery_codeBench_for ARM_GNU_Linux`, which Eclipse probably may not manage.

4. At the **Add to PATH** step, check either **Modify PATH for current user** or **Modify PATH for all users**. This allows the installer to change the windows environment variable **PATH** to include the location of the CodeBench Lite compiler.

5. Keep clicking on the **Next** buttons, and use the default options to continue. Once complete, a summary is displayed to confirm a successful install.

Verifying the installation

When the installation finishes, navigate to the installation folder (here, `C:\CodeSourcery`) on your host PC; you will see the files that have been installed. The key files are the executables of cross-compilers, which are in the subfolder bin (that is, `C:\CodeSourcery\bin`). The following table lists these core files:

Assembler:	arm-none-linux-gnueabi-as.exe
C compiler:	arm-none-linux-gnueabi-gcc.exe
C linker:	arm-none-linux-gnueabi-gcc.exe
C++ linker:	arm-none-linux-gnueabi-g++.exe
Archiver:	arm-none-linux-gnueabi-ar.exe
Debugger:	arm-none-linux-gnueabi-gdb.exe

Verifying the compiler

You can test that the CodeBench Lite cross-compiler is set up correctly, by running the following command at Windows' cmd window:

```
> arm-none-linux-gnueabi-gcc -v
```

If everything goes well, you will see that the last line of the screen output contains something like `Sourcery CodeBench Lite 2013.05-24`. Congratulations, you have successfully installed the CodeBench Lite cross-compiler on Windows 7.

> For experienced developers, you may now compile your C/C++ source code to get an ARM-compatible executable file in command windows. For example, you can build an executable file from a main `.c` source file (for example, a `Hello World!` program) by typing the following command on a Windows cmd window:
>
> ```
> > arm-none-linux-gnueabi-gcc main.c
> ```
>
> By default, the output executable file is `a.out` that is ready to run on the BeagleBoard. You can log in to your BeagleBoard, copy the file, and run it at your BeagleBoard.

Mac and Linux users

The Mentor Graphics Sourcery CodeBench Lite cross-complier for Windows has been proved to be very robust, and have very positive user experiences. CodeBench Lite is also available for a Linux PC. The installation procedure on Linux is similar to that on Windows.

Unfortunately, Sourcery CodeBench is not available for Apple's Mac OS X environment. However, some consultancy companies (such as Carlson-Minot Inc.) provide a free Mac version of Sourcery CodeBench Lite to the open source community. Please see `http://www.carlson-minot.com/mac-os-x-cross-toolchains/mac-os-x-cross-toolchain-faqs`.

> **Downloading the example code**
>
> You can download the example code files for all Packt books you have purchased from your account at `http://www.packtpub.com`. If you purchased this book elsewhere, you can visit `http://www.packtpub.com/support` and register to have the files e-mailed directly to you.

Installing Eclipse IDE on Windows 7

Eclipse is an open source IDE for various platforms including Windows 7. You can edit source code, compile source files, build and debug programs in Eclipse. Installing an Eclipse IDE on Windows 7, and configuring it for BeagleBoard will be done in three steps:

- Installing Eclipse IDE for C/C++ Developers
- Installing **GNU ARM Eclipse Plug-in** for easy project management
- Installing **Remote System Explorer** (**RSE**) Plug-in for remote file management and remote debugging

Installing Eclipse IDE for C/C++ Developers on Windows 7 is straightforward, and there have been many instructions and tutorials on the Internet and YouTube. You can go to the **Eclipse Downloads** page at `http://www.eclipse.org/downloads/`, click on **Eclipse IDE for C/C++ Developers**, select one of the packages (for example, **Indigo Packages**), and then follow the instructions and tutorials to complete the installation. In this book, we suppose the Eclipse is installed at `C:\eclipse`, and set the Eclipse Workspace (a working directory storing your projects and files) to `D:\Beagle\myWorkSpace`.

Installing the GNU ARM Eclipse plugin

To make project management and the cross-compilation procedure simple, we will use a plugin tool called GNU ARM Eclipse that supports the C/C++ development for ARM processors, following these steps:

1. If not already open, launch the Eclipse IDE by running the `eclipse.exe` file.
2. From the Eclipse menu bar, select **Help** | **Install New Software** to open the **Available Software** dialog (as shown). In the dialog window, do the following:

    1. Copy the URL `http://gnuarmeclipse.sourceforge.net/updates` into the **Work with** field followed by pressing *Enter*.

2. Wait for a while, the **CDT GNU Cross Development Tools** item will appear in the available software box. Expand it and tick **GNU ARM C/C++ Development Support**, as shown in the following screenshot:

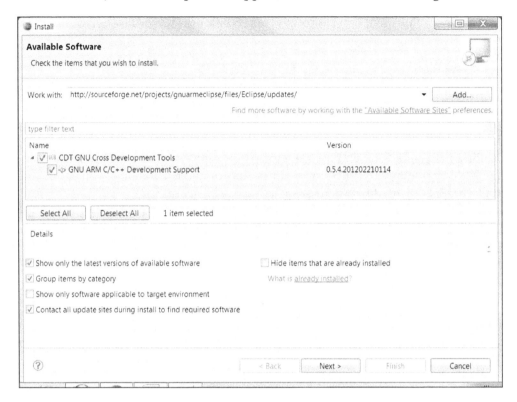

3. Click on the **Finish** button to complete the installation of the GNU ARM Eclipse plugin.

Installing Remote System Explorer (RSE)

RSE is an Eclipse plugin that provides a toolkit allowing you to connect to and work with a remote target system, that is, the BeagleBoard. It simplifies downloading files to and editing files on the BeagleBoard within the Eclipse IDE. For example, you can open a terminal, and log in to the BeagleBoard, look at remote files on the BeagleBoard at the terminal within Eclipse, transfer files between the host PC and the BeagleBoard, execute Linux commands, and, most attractively, debug the BeagleBoard program remotely within Eclipse.

Similar to installing the GNU ARM plugin, the simplest way to get RSE is via Eclipse's graphic user interface, following these steps:

1. In Eclipse, choose **Help | Install New Software** to open the software installation dialog; see the following screenshot.

2. In the **Work with** dropdown list, select the item **--All Available Sites--**.

3. In the **type filter text** field, type **remote**. After a while, depending on your Internet speed, a list of available software is displayed in the box.

4. Under the category **General Purpose Tools**, tick the following three items (as shown in the following screenshot).

    ○ **Dynamic Languages Toolkit - Remote Development Support**

    ○ **Remote System Explorer End-User Runtime**

    ○ **Remote System Explorer User Actions**

5. Click on **Next** to continue, accept the licenses, then **Finish** to restart Eclipse.

Connecting to a BeagleBoard in RSE

In Eclipse, choose **Windows | Open Perspective | Other** to open the **Open Perspective** window, where you can find an item called **Remote System Explorer**. Select it and click on **OK** to open the RSE perspective, which opens up a **Remote Systems** view at the left panel within Eclipse. By default, the **Remote Systems** view contains one item, **Local**, which is for the local file system on your host PC.

 You can switch among various perspectives by choosing **Window | Open Perspective | Other** to open the **Open Perspective** window. Then select the one you want to open. You can easily switch them by clicking on one of the perspective icons at the up-right corner of Eclipse.

To view the files on the BeagleBoard, follow the steps to create a connection to the BeagleBoard:

1. If your BeagleBoard is not already booted, power it on, and have your host PC connected to the BeagleBoard via an Ethernet network or an Ethernet cable.

2. You also need your BeagleBoard's IP address. In case you forgot it, press the **USER** button on the Beagleboard to hear the BeagleBoard speak its IP address. See section *Configuring the Beagleboard and Installing PuTTY* in *Chapter 2, Installing Linux on the BeagleBoard*.

3. In the **Remote Systems** view, right-click and select **New | Connection** from the context menu. In the **New Connection** dialog, choose **SSH only** from the **Select Remote System Type** list. And click on **Next** to open the configuration dialog (see the following figure):

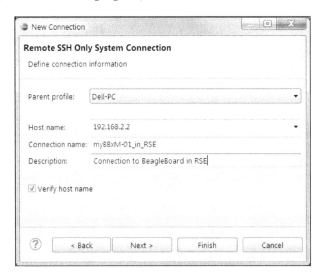

4. In the **Host name** input box, enter the IP address of your BeagleBoard, for example, `192.168.2.2`.

> If you prefer to use a host name instead of the IP address, you can edit the file `C:\windows\System32\drivers\etc\host` (please note, no extension name) on your Windows 7 host PC, and assign the hostname with an IP address by adding one line at the end of the file. For instance, `192.168.2.2 myBeagleBoard`.
>
> Save the host file and you now can use `myBeagleBoard` in the **Host Name** field.

5. Enter a connection name, in this example, **myBBxM-01_in_RSE**. This name will display in the connection tree in your **Remote System** view and must be unique; it will be used in remote debugging in the future.

6. Click on **Finish** and you will see that a new item, **myBBxM-01_in_RSE**, appears in the **Remote System** view. Right-click on the item **myBBxM-01_in_RSE** and select **Connect**. If it is the first time you connect to your BeagleBoard, you will be asked for username and password. Use the default user account with user name `ubuntu`, and the password `temppwd`. Click on **OK** to finish.

7. You may get some warning messages of failure in authenticity, or creating host files; click on **Yes** to continue the connection.

Once the connection is created, you can launch a terminal in RSE perspective to verify the connection. Right-click on **Ssh Terminals** under **Remote System** (here, it is **myBBxM-01_in_RSE**), and click on **Launch Terminal**. Then a tabbed **Terminals** window will appear at the bottom panel of Eclipse. In the tabbed **Terminals** window, you can try various Linux commands to view the files on the BeagleBoard, for example, `ls`, `pwd`, and so on. See the following figure:

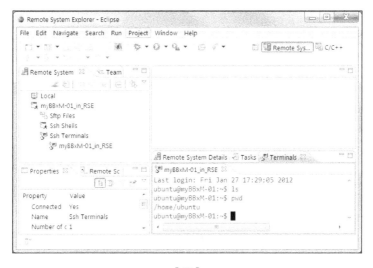

The SFTP function provided by RSE also allows you to manage remote files on the BeagleBoard within the graphic Eclipse IDE. In the **Remote System** view (see the preceding screenshot). You can create/copy/rename/delete files easily. You can also transfer files between your host PC (shown as **Local** at the top of the tree in the **Remote System** view) and your BeagleBoard.

Build your first Hello World! program

Now the cross-compiler and the Eclipse IDE for BeagleBoard have been set up on Windows 7 and we are going to write our first program, a classic `Hello World!`, on the Eclipse IDE, build it to get an executable program, and then run it on the BeagleBoard.

Creating your first project in Eclipse

Before we start typing code, we need to create a project so that we can easily manage the source files and configure the compilation options. Follow the steps to create your first C project:

1. Switch the Eclipse IDE into C/C++ perspective.

2. Create a C project. From the menu bar, select **File | New | C Project**. In the **C project** window, type in a project name (for example, `helloworld`). On the left panel of **Project Type**, select **Empty Project** under **ARM Cross Target Application**. On the right panel of **Toolchains**, select **ARM Windows GCC (Sourcery G++ Lite)**, and click on the **Finish** button. Then a project is created and a new folder `helloworld`, named after the project name, is created in your Eclipse workspace (here, it is `D:\Beagle\myWorkSpace`). As a result, an icon of an opened folder is displayed in the **Project Explorer** panel to represent both the project and the folder.

3. Create a source file (`main.c`). From the **File** menu, select **File | New | Source File**. In the **New Source File** dialog, specify the source folder as the project folder (that is, `helloworld`). In the **Source file** field, type the name of the source file, that is, `main.c`. Use the default option **Default C source template** in the **Template** field. Click on the **Finish** button.

4. Double-click on the `main.c` file in **Project Explorer** to start writing code in Eclipse's built-in text editor. Type the following code and save it into `main.c`:

```c
#include "stdio.h"
int main(void) {
  printf("Hello World!\n");
  return 0;
}
```

This file will be saved in the project folder, which is, in this example, `D:\Beagle\myWorkSpace\helloworld\main.c`.

Configuring the cross-compiler and the C/C++ build

Select and right-click on the project **helloworld** in **Project Explorer**, and then select **Properties** from the context menu. A new window **Properties for helloword** opens, where we will configure the parameters for the CodeBench Lite cross-compiler. In the left panel of the opened dialog window, navigate to **C/C++ Build | Settings**. In the right panel of **Settings**, click on the **Tool Settings** tab and do the following configuration for the respective fields:

- **Target Processor**
    - Processor: **cortex-a8**
    - Thumb (**-mthumb**): *checked*
- **Debugging**
    - **Debug format**: Toolchain Default
- **Additional Tools**
    - **Create Flash Image**: *unchecked*
- **ARM Sourcery Windows GCC C Assembler**
    - **Command**: `arm-none-linux-gnueabi-as`
- **ARM Sourcery Windows GCC C Compiler**
    - **Command**: `arm-none-linux-gnueabi-as`
- **ARM Sourcery Windows GCC C Linker**
    - **Command**: `arm-none-linux-gnueabi-gcc`
    - **General**: **Do not use standard start files**: *unchecked*
- **ARM Sourcery Windows GNU Create Flash Image**
    - **Command**: `arm-none-linux-gnueabi-objcopy`
- **ARM Sourcery Windows GNU Create Flash Listing**
    - **Command**: `arm-none-linux-gnueabi-objdump`
- **ARM Sourcery Windows GNU Create Print Size**
    - **Command**: `arm-none-linux-gnueabi-size`

The following figure shows the screenshot of setting **Target Processor** to **cortex-a8**. More details and screenshots of these configurations can be found at `http://dl.dropboxusercontent.com/u/3979723/dxw/projects/MatlabCodeGen4BeagleBoard/3_Helloworld_at_Beagleboard.htm#5`.

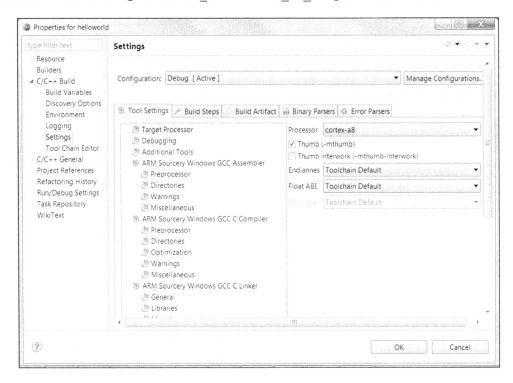

 In **ARM Sourcery Windows GCC C Linker | General**, the option **Do not use standard start files** must be unchecked, so that the gcc linker will not use the option `-nostartfiles` when creating the executable file. Otherwise, you will get a warning while compiling stating: `Cannot find entry symbol _start`.

It is also worth checking the `include` directories of the C Compiler. In the **Project Properties** window, go to **C/C++ General | Paths and Symbols | Includes Tab | Languages | GNU C**; the list of include directories should contain the directories as shown in the following screenshot. If not, please click on the **Add** button to add paths manually, shown as follows:

Click on the **Apply** button, and/or the **OK** buttons to finish the configuration.

Compiling our application

Now that we have set up the Sourcery CodeBench Lite cross-compiler, we can compile our source code to get an executable program.

From the Eclipse window, select **Project | Build All**. Alternatively, type the short keys *Ctrl+B* to build the project. The Sourcery CodeBench Lite cross-compiler will now compile our main.c file, and link it with the Linux C libraries, finally outputting a binary file called helloworld.elf. Once the compilation completes successfully, you will see the output information on the **Console** window (tabbed in the lower panel within the Eclipse IDE).

```
Problems  Tasks  Console ⊠    Properties  Git Repositories  History  Error Log
CDT Build Console [helloworld]
Finished building: ../main3.c
' '
'Building target: helloworld.elf'
'Invoking: ARM Sourcery Windows GCC C Linker'
arm-none-linux-gnueabi-gcc -Wl,-Map,helloworld.map -mcpu=cortex-a8 -mthumb -g3 -o
"helloworld.elf"  ./main3.o
'Finished building target: helloworld.elf'
' '
'Invoking: ARM Sourcery Windows GNU Create Listing'
arm-none-linux-gnueabi-objdump -h -S helloworld.elf > "helloworld.lst"
'Finished building: helloworld.lst'
' '
'Invoking: ARM Sourcery Windows GNU Print Size'
arm-none-linux-gnueabi-size  --format=berkeley helloworld.elf
   text    data     bss     dec     hex filename
   1056     292       4    1352     548 helloworld.elf
'Finished building: helloworld.siz'
' '

**** Build Finished ****
```

In the **Project Explorer** view, you will find some new folders and files under your project helloworld. Navigate and open the subfolder Debug; you will find the executable binary file hellowrold.elf, object files (for example, main.o), and a makefile.

So we have compiled our source file, and got the ARM-compatible executable file. However, the executable cannot run on our Windows host PC, as it is for ARM processors. The next task is to copy this file to the BeagleBoard on which we will run the program.

Transferring program files to a BeagleBoard

With the aid of RSE, you can not only manage the files on BeagleBoard within Eclipse easily (for example, create/copy/rename/delete files), but also transfer files between your Windows PC and the BeagleBoard.

From the **Project Explorer** view in Eclipse, navigate to **helloworld | Debug | helloworld.elf**. Right-click on the `helloworld.elf` file, and select **copy** from the context menu.

Switch to the RSE perspective by selecting **Window | Open Perspective | Other | Remote System Explorer**. In the **Remote System** view, now navigate to the remote system of your BeagleBoard, and select **Sftp Files | My Home** (which is the directory \home\ubuntu on your BeagleBoard). Right-click and select **Paste** to copy the `helloworld.elf` into your BeagleBoard.

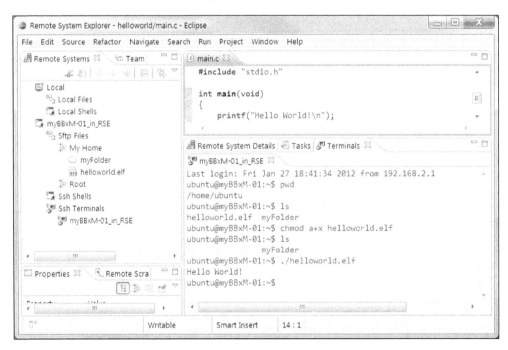

Running programs on the BeagleBoard

To run the program \home\ubuntu\helloworld.elf on the BeagleBoard, we need to launch a **Terminals** window, and log in. In the **Remote Systems** view, right-click on **Ssh Terminal**, and select **Launch Terminal**. Then a new tabbed window titled **Terminals** appears in the lower panel within the Eclipse IDE, displaying the command prompt on the BeagleBoard, as shown in the preceding screenshot.

In the **Terminals** window, enter the ls command to list the files in the current directory /home/ubuntu. You will see your executable file helloworld.elf. However, as default user ubuntu, you are not assigned the right to run the file. Enter the chmod a+x helloworld.elf command to give you the right execution. The last command is to run the program. Simply type: ./hellolworld.elf. You should now see a Hello World! greeting in the **Terminals** window (see the preceding screenshot).

Congratulations! You have written your first application in Windows 7, cross-compiled it, and have run it on the BeagleBoard.

Running and debugging remotely with Eclipse

For experienced developers, you often want a powerful tool to debug your program when it is running on the BeagleBoard. Remote debugging is particularly useful when your application gets bigger and more complicated. With Eclipse, you can run and debug a BeagleBoard program remotely at your host computer.

On the BeagleBoard, you need to install **gdbserver**, if not already installed. In the Eclipse IDE, switch to the RSE perspective and launch a Terminal to BeagleBoard. In the the Terminal window, enter the sudo apt-get install gadserver command to install gdbserver. More details of the gdbserver package for Ubuntu (11.04 Natty Narwhal) can be found at www.ubuntuupdates.org/package/core/natty/universe/base/gdbserver.

On the host PC, you need to set up a remote debug configuration. In Eclipse, select **Run | Debug Configurations** to open a configuration dialog window where you can create and manage configurations. Follow these steps to set up the remote debug configuration:

1. Right-click on **C/C++ Remote Application**, and select **New** from the context menu to create a debug configuration.

In the main tab, at the **C/C++ Application** field, click on the **Search Project** button to find the executable file to be debugged (for example, `Debug/helloworld.elf`). In the **Connection** field, select the connection you have created for the BeagleBoard (for example, `myBBxM-01_in_RSE`). In the **Remote Absolute File Path for C/C++ Application** field, browse to or enter the directory and the filename where you want to upload the executable file on the BeagleBoard, for example: `/home/ubuntu/helloworld.elf`. In **Commands to execute before application**, enter `chmod a+x /home/ubuntu/helloworld.elf`. Click on **Apply**.

2. Click on the **Debugger** tab, in **GDB debugger** enter or browse to `C:\ CodeSourcery\bin\arm-none-linux-gnueabi-gdb.exe`.

3. Under the **Debugger** tab, select the **gdbserver Settings** tab. In **Port number**, enter a free TCP port (by default, `2345`).

4. Finish the configuration by clicking on **Apply**.

Now you can start debugging by clicking on the **Debug** button directly in the configuration window. If asked to **Confirm Perspective Switch**, click on **Yes**. Alternatively, you can start remote debugging from the Eclipse menu. Choose **Run | Debug As** or **Run | Debug History**, and select the remote debug configuration you just created earlier.

Eclipse should now upload `helloworld.elf` automatically to the BeagleBoard and begin remote debugging. By default, you should see the program stopped at the first line of the main function. Press *F6* on the host PC's keyboard and the program will advance one line. The print output should appear in the **Console** tab in the lower panel of Eclipse.

On the BeagleBoard, you can verify that your `helloworld.elf` program is running, by viewing the active processes. At the **Terminals** window, tabbed in the lower panel of Eclipse, enter the `top` command, and you will see your `helloworld` process.

Summary

In this chapter, we have set up our Windows 7 PC with the CodeBench Lite cross-compiler and an Eclipse IDE to write and compile our BeagleBoard C/C++ application. Then we configured the Eclipse IDE to run and debug the BeagleBoard application remotely at our Windows 7 PC.

Eclipse and its plugins (for example, RSE) have an extensive number of features which are out of the scope of discussion for this book. However, you can find a comprehensive guide to the IDE on the Eclipse website:

- `http://www.eclipse.org/resources/?category=Getting Started.`
- `https://sites.google.com/site/learningeclipsearm/home.`
- `http://www.tutorialspoint.com/eclipse/index.htm.`

We have also written our first C application and learned how to compile code, transfer files to the BeagleBoard, and run and debug applications on the BeagleBoard remotely. Following this, you have understood the workflow of embedded software development for BeagleBoard. We can move onto our first MATLAB/Simulink project for rapid prototyping.

4
Automatic Code Generation

Throughout the previous chapters, we have set up our BeagleBoard and the cross-platform development environment at our Windows 7 PC.

In this chapter, we will look at automatic code generation by MATLAB/Simulink for rapid prototyping. Automatic code generation and visual programming are fundamentally changing the way engineers work. In this chapter, instead of typing lines of C code manually, we develop our applications either in high-level scripts or in graphical programming and generate executable standalone applications.

This chapter serves as the introduction to automatic C code generation, graphical programming, and modular raid prototyping. The following two approaches of automatic code generation will be explored:

1. We will first demonstrate how to generate C code and BeagleBoard executables from MATLAB scripts.

2. Then we will develop a program for playing music in Simulink by graphically manipulating function blocks rather than coding textually. And then run the executables as standalone applications on the BeagleBoard.

Through these two projects, you will experience the power of MATLAB and Simulink in terms of automatic code generation and graphical programming.

MATLAB code generation

First up, we are going to look at a simple MATLAB program calculating mean values of 10 numbers. Then we will set a code generation project in MATLAB to generate C code from the MATLAB program and compile the C code in Eclipse.

MATLAB and m-language

MATLAB provides a very powerful high-level programming language, known as m-language or m-script, for numerical computation and data processing. We are going to go through the following steps and quickly take a look at a very simple program written in the MATLAB m-language:

1. Launch MATLAB and create a folder (for example, `C:\myMatlab`) as your working folder to save your MATLAB code and project files.

2. Navigate to your working folder that we just created, through **File** | **New** | **Function** to create an empty MATLAB script file `calcavg.m`. Type in the following code in the text editor and save it to `calcavg.m`:

    ```
    function avg = calcavg(a) %#codegen
    avg=mean(a);
    ```

    Here, variable `a` is the input argument that indeed is an array storing 10 numbers; variable `avg` is the return value of the average of these 10 numbers. From a math standpoint, variable `a` is a vector of length 10 and `avg` is scalar. The simple example program calculates the mean values of these 10 numbers.

    `mean()` is a basic function provided in MATLAB and `mean(a)` returns the mean values of all the elements in vector `a`.

As shown in the simple example, the main advantage of MATLAB is that a data processing algorithm requiring tens or hundreds of lines of C code can be achieved with a few lines of MATLAB.

Code generation workflow in MATLAB

Once we get an idea about the applications, the first step in the code generation process is to prepare the algorithms in MATLAB. Then we test our algorithm in the MATLAB environment. If the algorithm works well, we generate C/C++ code from the m-scripts by making use of the **MATLAB Coder** toolbox. Then we compile the C code in Eclipse to get the executable and test it as a standalone application on the BeagleBoard. If we are satisfied with its performance on the BeagleBoard, we can deploy the software. If we are not satisfied, we go back to the m-scripts to improve the algorithm's performance.

Selecting a compiler for MATLAB Coder

MATLAB Coder requires a compiler for code generation. Various compilers can be used by MATLAB Coder and, by default, an LCC compiler comes with MATLAB. However, when we first use MATLAB Coder to generate code, we have to explicitly tell the MATLAB Coder which compiler is to be used for code generation.

If you have not already set up a compiler in MATLAB by `mex -setup` command, you can type command `mex -setup` in the MATLAB command window to select the default LCC compiler for MATLAB Coder.

When prompted, type *y* to confirm that you are going to find a compiler. And all the compilers available on your host PC will be listed with a number ID.

Then select the LCC-win32 compiler by entering its number ID. For example, type 1 followed by pressing the *Enter* key. And type *y* to confirm your selection.

When the configuration of the compiler is finished, some information will be shown in the command window to suggest a successful selection.

C/C++ code generation with MATLAB Coder

The tool we are going to use for code generation is called MATLAB Coder. To generate C code from function `calcavg.m`, we need to create a MATLAB Coder project.

From the MATLAB main menu, navigate to **File | New | Code Generation Project**. A **Matlab Coder Project** dialog box opens: enter a name for the project (for example, we use the name `mycalcavg`), set the folder to location `C:\myMatlab`, and click on **OK**. As a result, MATLAB Coder creates a project file `mycalcavg.prj`. Follow these steps to generate the C code:

1. A new window **MATLAB Coder: MEX Function** opens. Click on **Add files** in the **Overview** tab to add the m-file (`calcavg.m`) into the project.

2. Specify thetype of input argument. Because C uses static typing, MATLAB Coder has to determine the properties of all variables in the MATLAB files at compiling time. Therefore, we must specify the properties (type and size) of the function's input variables before you compile the file.

In the **Overview** tab, the type of the input parameter a was classified as undefined. Click on the gear icon next to the input parameter a, and select **Edit Type...** from the context drop-down menu. A new window opens to define the parameter type: set the **Class** field to **double** and the **Size** field to 1 x 10. Click on the gear button next to the **Size** field and select **Mark Sizes Variable**. Leave the checkbox of **Complex** unchecked. Click on **OK** to finish the parameter type definition and the **Overview** tab will look like the following screenshot:

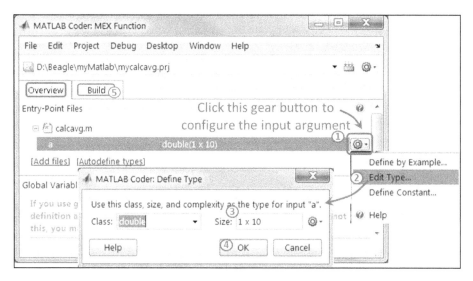

In the previous example, the input variable a is a 1 x 10 vector and we specify its type as double with size of 1 x 10.

MATLAB Coder also supports input arguments with variable size. For example, if we set the argument type to 1X:10 (please note the colon between x and 10), it means the size of argument is variable with upper bound to 1 x 10.

Now we can generate C code by a few clicks. Follow these steps to generate code:

1. Switch to the **Build** tab in the **MATLAB Coder Project** dialog.
2. Select **C/C++ Static Library** from the **Output type** drop-down list. By default, the output file is the same as the m file, that is, calcavg.
3. Check the checkbox **Generate code only**.
4. Click on the **Build** button to generate the C code.

The **Build progress** dialog box will appear. Once it is finished, you will get a success message and a link to a code generation report. If you want, click on the link to view the report in which you can easily navigate the C files generated.

The generated C files are located in the subfolder `<WorkingFolder>\codegen\lib\` `<matlabfilename>` under your current folder, where `<WorkingFolder>` represents the current MATLAB working folder (that is, `C:\myMatlab`) and `<matlabfilename>` represents the name of the m-file for code generation (that is, `mycalcavg`).

The generated code include several C source and header files. In particular, the two source/header files are as follows:

- `calcavg.h/.c`: The core function of average calculation is declared in the header file and defined in `calcavg.c`.

```
real_T calcavg(const real_T a[10])
{
  real_T y;
  int32_T k;
  /* UNTITLED2 Summary of this function goes here */
  /* Detailed explanation goes here */
  y = a[0];
  for (k = 0; k < 9; k++) {
    y += a[k + 1];
  }
  return y / 10.0;
}
```

  As you can see, the generated C function `calcavg()` is to calculate the average of 10 numbers, which is what we expect. The variable type `real_T` is defined as `typedef double time_T;` in file `rtwtypes.h` in the same folder.

- `calcavg_initialize.h/.c`: These two files declare and define the initialization function `void calcavg_initialize(void)`. We need to initialize something by referring to the function `calcavg_initialize()` before we make the first call to `calcavg()`.

Creating BeagleBoard applications in Eclipse

In most cases, the algorithm developed in MATLAB is part of a larger application and the generated C code is in the format of a static library. Once the C code is generated, we will take the generated code and integrate it with the rest of the application.

In this section, we will integrate the generated code into an Eclipse project and make use of **Eclipse IDE** and **CodeBench Lite** to create the executable for BeagleBoard.

Creating an Eclipse project for BeagleBoard applications

We now create a new blank C/C++ project for the BeagleBoard in Eclipse and include the generated C code into the project by following the steps:

1. Create a new Eclipse C project targeting the BeagleBoard with the project name mycalcavgC. We need an ARM Cross Target Application C/C++ project. Navigate to **File | New | C project** to open the **C Project** dialog. Select **ARM Cross Target Application** as the project type and **ARM Windows GCC (Sourcery G++ Lite)** for toolchains. Then click on **Finish**.

2. Configure the project mycalcavgC for using the CodeBench Lite compiler. More details of how to create and configure an Eclipse project for BeagleBoard were discussed in the section *Create your first project in Eclipse*, in *Chapter 3, C/C++ Development with Eclipse on Windows*.

3. Include the generated code into the project. This is done by a **link folder** that links to the folder at which the C code generated by MATLAB Coder are stored. Right click on the project **mycalcavgC** and navigate to **Properties | C/C++ General | Paths and Symbols**: select the **Source Location** tab, as shown in the following screenshot. Click on **Link Folder...** to add the source folder C:\myMatlab\codegen\lib\calcavg into the Eclipse project. Once it is done, you will see a new source folder **/mycalcavgC/calcavg** in the tree of **Source folders on build path**, as shown in the following screenshot. The link folder **calcavg** will also appear in your project explorer tab.

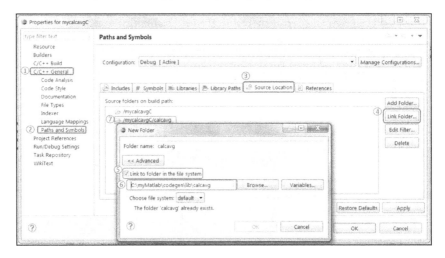

4. Create a source file (`main.c`) and set up the main function to kick off the application. The main function performs basic actions to take the input from the user, exercise the code generated from MATLAB, and display the results.

```
#include <stdio.h>
#include "calcavg.h"
#include "calcavg_initialize.h"
int main(void)
{ int i;
  double x[10]; // ten numbers
  double y; // the average of ten numbers

  calcavg_initialize();
  printf("Please enter ten numbers separated by
    space:\n");
  for (i=0;i<9;i++) scanf("%lf ", &x[i]);
  scanf("%lf", &x[9]);

  y=calcavg(x); //call matlab generated code to calculate
    avg

  printf("The numbers are: \n   ");
  for (i=0;i<10;i++)  printf("%f ", x[i]);
  printf("\n");
  printf("and their average is %f\n",y);
  return 0;
}
```

5. Build the project to get the executable for the BeagleBoard. From the Eclipse menu, navigate to **Project | Build All** (or hit the short key *Ctrl + B*) to build the project. You will get the executable `mycalcavgC.elf` at folder `Debug` under your project directory.

Running the executable at the BeagleBoard

We have got the executable `mycalcavgC.elf`, and we are going to run it on the at BeagleBoard remotely through the **Remote System Explorer** (**RSE**) in Eclipse. We need to first create a new Run configuration for our project. From the Eclipse main menu, navigate to **Run | Run Configurations** to open a dialog window, where we set the configuration to run `mycalcavgC.elf`. The configuration tells Eclipse how to run the application on the BeagleBoard. See the following screenshot.

We first select the type of configuration as **C/C++ Remote Application**, and then click on the new button to create a new configuration. We can change the name of the configuration and select the connection to **myBBxM-01_in_RSE**, which is a remote connection we created during the installation of RSE. Click on **Browse** to find the project mycalcavgC and tell Eclipse that the C/C++ application we want to run is mycalcavgC.elf, located at the project's Debug subfolder as shown in the following screenshot:

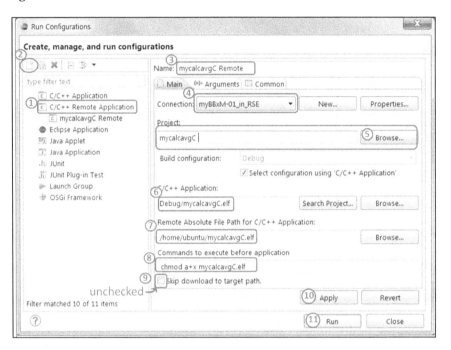

We also need to specify which executable we want to run remotely on the BeagleBoard. By default, we set it to /home/ubuntu/mycalcavgC.elf. As a result, the output file of the compiler Debug/mycalcavgC.elf on the host PC will be first downloaded to /home/ubuntu/mycalcavgC.elf. The Linux command chmod a+x mycalcavgC.elf will be executed remotely to give users the right to run mycalcavgC.elf. It is common to uncheck the checkbox of **Skip download to target path.** Check it unless you want to update the executable on the BeagleBoard.

Finally, click on the **Apply** button to make the configuration effective, and then click on the **Run** button to run the application on the BeagleBoard. You will see the output at the remote **Console** tab in the lower panel of Eclipse as shown in the following screenshot:

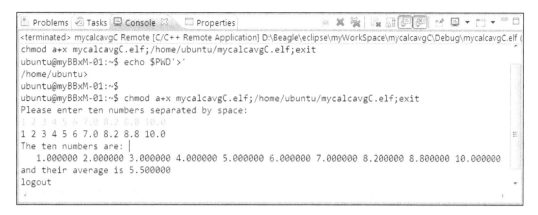

```
Problems    Tasks    Console    Properties
<terminated> mycalcavgC Remote [C/C++ Remote Application] D:\Beagle\eclipse\myWorkSpace\mycalcavgC\Debug\mycalcavgC.elf (
chmod a+x mycalcavgC.elf;/home/ubuntu/mycalcavgC.elf;exit
ubuntu@myBBxM-01:~$ echo $PWD'>'
/home/ubuntu>
ubuntu@myBBxM-01:~$
ubuntu@myBBxM-01:~$ chmod a+x mycalcavgC.elf;/home/ubuntu/mycalcavgC.elf;exit
Please enter ten numbers separated by space:
1 2 3 4 5 6 7.0 8.2 8.8 10.0
1 2 3 4 5 6 7.0 8.2 8.8 10.0
The ten numbers are: |
    1.000000 2.000000 3.000000 4.000000 5.000000 6.000000 7.000000 8.200000 8.800000 10.000000
and their average is 5.500000
logout
```

Congratulations! You have written a data processing algorithm in MATLAB, generated C code, integrated the automatically generated code into an Eclipse project, and run it as a standalone application on the BeagleBoard.

For experienced users, you may want to log into the BeagleBoard through PuTTY and you will see is been an executable file in the Ubuntu home folder. Simply type the command ./mycalcavgC.elf at the PuTTY terminal window to run the application.

Simulink code generation

Simulink, a graphical tool for modeling and simulating systems, provides an interactive graphical programming environment and enables rapid prototyping to explore design ideas at an early stage. An attracting feature of Simulink is that you can tune parameters of your design "on the fly" and immediately see what happens on the BeagleBoard, for "what if" exploration.

There are two major kinds of elements in Simulink, namely function blocks and signal lines. As a graphical programming language, a program is presented as a block diagram (referred to as a Simulink model) where blocks are connected by lines. In this section, we will build a simple program by creating a Simulink model and then run that model to play a music file (a *.wav file) on the BeagleBoard. We will also adjust the parameters of the model (in this example model, it is the volume or balance) on the fly.

A Simulink model of a music player

The Simulink model of the music player we are going to build is shown in the following screenshot:

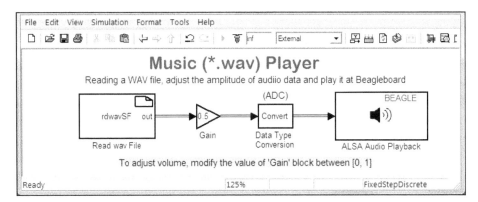

The model consists of five blocks in three groups:

- Data acquisition (**Read wav File** block)
- Data processing (**Gain** and **Data Type Conversion** blocks)
- Data output (**ALSA Audio Playback** block)

The **Read wav File** block is a source block that opens the music file on the BeagleBoard and reads the digital audio data. The **Gain** block takes the digital audio data as input and modifies the data's amplitude by multiplying its gain value. Varying the gain value between [0, 1], we can adjust the amplitude of the audio stream. The result of product could be a decimal fraction (analog value) and we need a **Data Type Conversion** block to convert it into a digital value. This block works like an **analog-to-digital converter** (**ADC**). Finally, the modified digital audio data is transferred to the **ALSA Audio Playback** block that drives the BeagleBoard audio hardware to make sounds. The **ALSA Audio Playback** block is called a sink block, as the data achieves its final destination and is converted into other forms.

From the perspective of software, the source and sink blocks are hardware drivers interfacing with the BeagleBoard hardware. The built-in BeagleBoard support package has an integrated **ALSA Audio Playback** block that drives the sound hardware through the open-source **Advanced Linux Sound Architecture** (**ALSA**) framework. We will develop our own device driver block of **Read wav File** to open and read a .wav music file.

Building the Simulink model

Building a model is done by bringing up a new Simulink model window and creating a block diagram through a series following these steps:

1. Drag a block from **Library** and place it in your model.

2. Double-click on the block to open its properties window, where the block's parameters are configured to fit our system and requirements.

3. Finally, the blocks are connected with signal/data lines to complete the model.

If you have already launched MATLAB, entering command `simulink` will start Simulink and the **Simulink Library Browser** window will appear.

To create a new model, you can navigate to **File | New | Model**, and a new window opens with an empty model. Alternatively, you can open the example model **Beagleboard_Player** by double-clicking on the `Beagleboard_Player.mdl` that can be found in this chapter's source code folder.

The **ALSA Audio Playback** block is in the folder of **Simulink Support Package for BeagleBoard Hardware**, which can be found at the bottom of the library tree, in the left panel of the **Simulink Library Brower**. When you place it into your model, you can double-click on it to verify its parameters.

The **Gain** and **Data Type Conversion** block are in the **Math Operations** subfolder under the **Simulink** folder in the library tree. Once you've added the **Gain** block into your model, double-click on it and set its field **Gain** to a number between [0, 1], which will be used to adjust the amplitude of the audio data.

The **Read wav File** block is an **S-Function Builder** block. This block is a so-called "device driver block" that performs specific functions (that is, opening and reading the audio file from the BeagleBoard's microSD card). The procedure of developing a custom Simulink device driver block will be discussed in detail in the following section.

Writing a Simulink device driver block for a BeagleBoard

In this section, we will make use of the S-Function Builder block, which is under **User Defined Functions** in the Simulink library, to generate **S-Functions (system-functions)**. An S-Function consists of a set of sub-functions describing the behavior of a dynamic system (that is, how the system's output is changed with response to the input). These sub-functions are organized into three groups and executed in three steps: taking input, updating states, and driving outputs.

For the purpose of developing a BeagleBoard driver block, we want the S-Function to actually perform a reading file operation on the BeagleBoard. The output of the S-function is the audio data streaming read from the WAV file. The file name (a character string) is regarded as a parameter to the S-Function. Thus, there is no need for input signals and state variables.

To begin with, we add an S-Function Builder block to our model from the Simulink library. Double-click on the block to open the configuration window (see the following screenshot), where we will follow these steps to develop our S-function:

1. The first step is to give a name to the S-Function by typing name in the input box of **S-function name**. In this example, we use `rdwav_SF` (for read WAV S-Function).

2. The first pane is called **Initialization**, where we set **sample mode** to `discrete`, set **sample time value** to `0.1`, and leave other configurations to the default value zero.

3. In the next **Data Properties** pane, perform the following configurations:

   ° Select the **Input ports** tab and click on the delete button to delete the input variable, as we do not need any input to this block.

   ° In the **Output Ports** tab, change **Dimension** to **2-D** and set **Rows** to `4410`, **Columns** to `2`, **Complexity** to **real**, and **Frame** to **on**, as shown in the following screenshot:

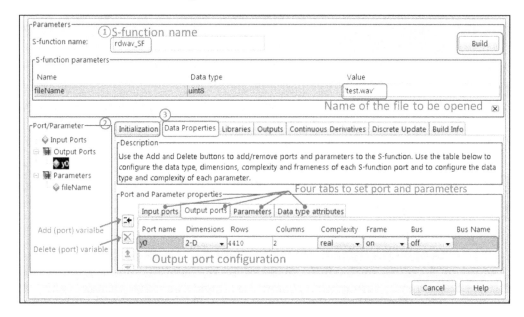

○ In the **Parameters** tab, add one parameter with **Parameter name** of `fileName`, **Data type** of `uint8`, and **Complexity** of `real`. You will see this parameter appears just below the **S-function name** field, at the top-half of the window. In its field **Value**, type in the name of the file to be opened, for example, `'test.wav'` (quoted by single quotation marks).

○ In the **Data type attributes** tab, set **Data type** of the output variable **y0** to `int16` and leave the other options at their default values.

4. In the **Libraries** pane, we include the source and header files used by our code. We only include three standard C libraries, as shown in the following screenshot. The preprocessor macros **#ifndef MATLAB_MEX_FILE** specify the conditional inclusion of these C libraries. The code typed in the **Libraries** pane will be placed directly at the beginning of the generated C file. Thus, it is common to make use of the **Library** pane to declare global variables (if you need), which will be accessible from the Update and Outputs functions as shown in the following screenshot:

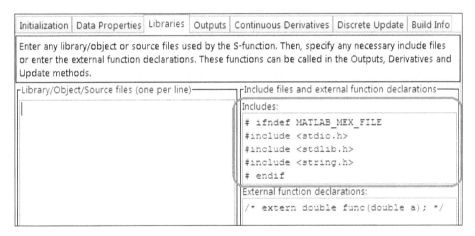

5. In the **Outputs** pane, write the following code as the block's output function:

```
/* Do nothing for mex file generation */
# ifndef MATLAB_MEX_FILE
static int firstOpenFile=1;
static FILE * pFile=NULL;
static short *dataframe;
static int nBytedataFrame;
```

```
int i, nByteRead, nSamPerFrame;
char *fName;
char wavheader[44];
int nChn, sampRate, bitPerSamp, datalen;

nSamPerFrame=4410; //One frame are 4410 samples for 0.1
                   //second

if (firstOpenFile==1)  // open file once at
                       // initialization
{ firstOpenFile=0;
  fName= (char *) malloc(p_width0+1);
  memcpy(fName,fileName,p_width0);
  fName[p_width0]=0x0;
  pFile=fopen(fName,"r");
  if (pFile==NULL){ printf("Open file %s failed.\n",
    fName);
    return;
    }
  // read wav file information
  fread(wavheader, 1, 44, pFile);
  nChn = (short) wavheader[22]+(wavheader[23]<<8);
  sampRate=*(int *)(&wavheader[24]);
  bitPerSamp = *(short *)(&wavheader[34]);

  // allocate nBytedataFrame bytes memory for data reading
  nBytedataFrame=nSamPerFrame*2*sizeof(short);
  dataframe= (short *) malloc(nBytedataFrame);
}
else{ // read one frame of data from was file
  nByteRead = fread(dataframe, 1, nBytedataFrame, pFile);
  if (nByteRead != nBytedataFrame)
  { //if file ends or any errors, go back to beginning
    fseek(pFile, 44, SEEK_SET);
    fread(dataframe, 1, nBytedataFrame, pFile);
  }
  //convert row-wise array data into column-wise framed
  //data
  for (i=0;i<nSamPerFrame;i++)
  { y0[i]=dataframe[i*2];
    y0[nSamPerFrame+i]=dataframe[i*2+1];
  }
}
# endif
```

The previous code consist of two parts: initialization (opening the specified file once) and repeated operation of reading 4410 samples of audio data from the file. We use a static variable to store the file handle to avoid frequent file opening. As we define an input parameter (`fileName`, `uint8`-type) to our S-Function, we can refer to `fileName` to get the file name. The S-Function Builder also provides an additional but implicit input parameter `p_width0` that represents how many characters (`uint8`) the first input parameter `fileName` has. It is worth noting that `fileName` is an array of `char`, rather than a `string`, and does not come with the string termination indicator (`0x00`). We have to manually pad a `0x00` to `fileName`. Furthermore, the input `fileName` will be declared as a constant input in the generated C code; we define a new variable `char *fName` for the purpose of padding the string terminator `0x00`.

In the file-reading part, once we read the desired amount of data into `dataframe`, it is a row-wise array in C. However, MATLAB/Simulink use column-wise arrays. We use a for-loop to convert the row-wise array into a column-wise array. Furthermore, when we reach the end of the file, we go back to the first audio data (44-byte offset from the file's beginning) and repeat reading the data again. As a result, the music will be played repeatedly. More details of the `*.wav` file format can be found at `https://ccrma.stanford.edu/courses/422/projects/WaveFormat/`.

6. The last (rightmost) pane is **Build Info**. Check the **Generate wrapper TLC** and uncheck the **Enable access to SimStruct** checkboxes. Enabling access to SimStruct will have the generated code include a header file `SimStruct.h`, which may be incompatible with your target hardware.

7. The final step is to generate C code for our block by clicking on the **Build** button. If everything goes well, we will get four files:

    ◦   A wrapper file (`rdwav_SF_wrapper.c`)
    ◦   A TLC file (`rdwav_SF.tlc`)
    ◦   An S-Function file (`rdwav_SF.c`)
    ◦   A MEX-file (`rdwav_SF.mexw32`)

    The most important file is the wrapper file, which contains the C code that you just typed in those configuration panes.

So far, we have built our own Simulink block that works as a hardware driver reading audio data from file `test.wav`. In execution, Simulink makes repeated calls during specific stages to each block in the model. As a result, the output function we just built will be called at the specified rate (0.1 second) to read the file and put recent audio data in the block's output. The audio file we are reading is a standard WAV file containing two channel stereo data, sampled at 44100 Hz with 16-bit per sample.

As we set our block's simulation interval to 0.1 second, every calling to our output function will acquire a frame of data containing the audio of 0.1 second, which are 4410 samples for each channel. More specifically, the output is a 4410 x 2 matrix (referred to as framed data) and each element of the matrix is of `int16` type corresponding to 16-bit per sample.

Configuring the model to run on a BeagleBoard

We have developed our Simulink model of a music player. Now we will configure the model to run on a BeagleBoard. Before we move on to the next step, it is worth checking that our host PC and BeagleBoard are connected via Ethernet. This can be done by launching the PuTTY utility and seeing if you can log into the BeagleBoard. You may press and release the **USER** button on the BeagleBoard to hear the BeagleBoard hardware speak its IP address.

From the main menu of our Simulink model window, navigate to **Tools | Run on Target hardware | Prepare to Run**. The target hardware information will be automatically populated. Check the **Enable External mode** option and leave the **TCP/IP port** parameter at its default value 17725. Your host PC will use this port to communicate with the BeagleBoard. Verify the IP address, username, and password. Then click on **OK**.

In the toolbar of the Simulink model window, set the simulation stop time to **inf** to run our model until we click on the pause or stop button. Save the model to finish the configuration.

For your convenience, a pre-configured model `Beagleboard_Player.mdl` is enclosed in this chapter's source code folder. It can be used as a template for future development.

Running the music player on the BeagleBoard

Before we start running our model, we need to put a WAV audio file named `test.wav` in the home directory (`/home/ubuntu`) on the BeagleBoard. An example audio file `test.wav` is included in this chapter's source code folder for convenience. You can download this file to the BeagleBoard easily through either the WinSCP or the RSE in Eclipse.

Now, navigate to **Tools | Run on Target Hardware | Run** to run the model on the BeagleBoard. It may take some time for the Simulink engine to prepare, compile, and download the model to the BeagleBoard. Once done, a system command window will open that shows the messages coming from our model running on the BeagleBoard. Please note that we have to explicitly select **Run on Target Hardware** to have our model run on the BeagleBoard.

You should now hear the music, which will be repeatedly played by the BeagleBoard. If you want to stop the music, click on the stop button (a black square).

Playing music without Simulink

When logging into the BeagleBoard at a PuTTY terminal or RSE terminal, you will find the executable file of your Simulink model at /home/ubuntu/$ModelName_rtt/ MW/ $ModelName, where $ModelName represents the main name of your *.mdl file, for example, /home/ubuntu/Beagleboard_Player_rtt/MW/Beagleboard_Player. In the home folder (/home/ubuntu) where you store the music file, enter the command ./Beagleboard_Player_rtt/MW/Beagleboard_Player, and you will play the music as well.

Tuning model parameters on the fly

In the model we just developed, we reduce the amplitude of audio data by an attenuation rate of 50 percent, which is regarded as a parameter by our model. When the model is running on the BeagleBoard hardware, the volume of music is fixed to half of the full scale. We may want to update the attenuation rate on the fly, so that we can change the volume when we are hearing the music. To accomplish this, follow these steps:

1. We can declare a variable (that is, attRatio) in the MATLAB base workspace to represent the attenuation rate and assign a value, say 0.1, to it. The command is attRatio=0.1.

2. In the Simulink model Beagleboard_Player, double-click on the **Gain** block and set the **gain** field to **attRatio**. This is to tell the Simulink block to take the value of the variable attRatio as its gain. When we assign different values to attRatio at the MATLAB command line, the gain of the **Gain** block will change and, in turn, the attenuation rate of audio data is changed. However, this treatment takes effect only when we start running the model. Every time we change the value of attRatio, we have to restart the model.

3. In order to tune the attenuation ratio on the fly without rebooting, once we change the value of attRatio at the MATLAB base workspace, we make a call to the MATLAB function set_param() in the MATLAB command window:

   ```
   set_param(bdroot,'SimulationCommand','update');
   ```

   where bdroot is an object representing the Simulink model that is currently running on the BeagleBoard. This command is to update the Simulink model (that is our Beagleboard_Player running on the target hardware) according to the current values of variables in MATLAB's base workspace.

A pre-configured model (`Beagleboard_Player2.mdl`) with the capability of tuning parameters on the fly is provided in this chapter's source code folder for your convenience.

Tuning model parameters through GUIs

You may also want to tune the parameters through a friendly graphic interface. MATLAB also provides utilities to develop custom **graphic user interfaces** (**GUIs**), eliminating the need to use extensive commands in the command line.

In this chapter's source code folder, you can find a Simulink model (`Beagleboard_Player3.mdl`) with associated GUIs (`balanceCtr.fig`, `balanceCtr.m`). When the `Beagleboard_Player3` model starts on the BeagleBoard, the GUI `balanceCtr` will start automatically, in which you can adjust the stereo's balance on the fly by varying the slider bars to change the attenuations of left and right channels individually, as shown in the following screenshot:

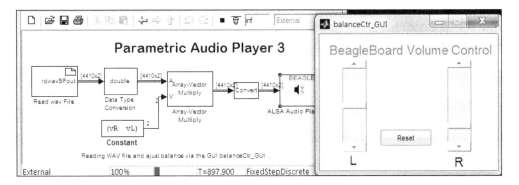

To understand how this works, open the example model file and navigate to **File | Model Properties** to open a dialog window. Select the **Callbacks** tab: under **InitFcn***, we use two commands, `vL=0.05; vR=0.05;` to set initial values to variables `vL` and `vR`, representing the attenuation ratio of the left and right channels, respectively. Under **StartFcn***, we invoke `balanceCtrl_GUI` to start the GUI window.

Other things to try

In order to explore the advances of rapid prototyping by Simulink graphical programming and parameter tuning on the fly, a revised parametric audio equalizer (`Beagleboard_PlayerEqualizer.mdl`) is included in the chapter's source folder. In this model, while you are listening to the music from the speaker connected to your BeagleBoard, you can adjust the parameters of the three band filters in the model and see what will happen immediately to the music you are hearing. You can easily enhance the bass components and reduce the high frequency parts, or vice versa.

Summary

This chapter showed two automatic code generation approaches: generating code from m script with MATLAB Coder and generating code from a Simulink model with the BeagleBoard built-in support in Simulink. A demo of a data-processing algorithm (averaging) is implemented in m script. Several audio processing demos demonstrate the advantages of MATLAB/Simulink-based rapid prototyping. In particular, we have learned how to build a custom hardware driver block for BeagleBoard.

We can move onto our first MATLAB/Simulink project for a more practical project, the rapid prototyping of a motion detector for a smart home.

5
Digital I/O and Serial Communication

In this chapter we will introduce how to utilize digital I/O and serial communication ports to drive external sensors, for example, an infrared (IR) sensor for motion detection in smart home applications. Driving sensors to collect data is an essential task in prototyping development. In this chapter's demo, an IR sensor is employed as the data acquisition input, driven by code that enables the system making use of the sensor data.

The following topics are discussed in detail:

- Voltage shifting: Voltage conversion between the BeagleBoard and external devices
- Digital I/O: Interfacing a device via the BeagleBoard's digital I/O
- Serial communication: Interfacing a device via the BeagleBoard's serial port
- Integration with data processing and control algorithms, and integrating a filtering algorithm when a motion is detected

Accordingly, we will demonstrate two different methods for driving sensors and acquiring data: using digital I/O in Simulink and writing textual code in C and MATLAB. Nonetheless, both of them can achieve the simple motivation of this book—rapid prototyping. However, the graphical one may be convenient for some people, since it can avoid code writing.

By the end of this chapter, you will be able to set up a simple home security system and extend the ability of this simple system as you wish.

IR sensor hardware

In the previous chapters, we focused the discussion on developing the environment and process for the BeagleBoard. However, for some applications, a single BeagleBoard is not enough, which means we usually need several external devices to work with the BeagleBoard to operate as a whole system. Usually we name an external device as **sensor**, if it mainly provides the information of the real-life world. Accordingly, we will name an external device as **actuator**, if it can affect the real-life world. Nonetheless, we will need a **driver** to power the external devices and obtain information from these external devices for the BeagleBoard as input to the processing algorithm.

A driver is a segment of code, which can be called in the form of lib or source code. These code will enable the user to access the internal and external hardware devices. In most scenarios the hardware vendor will provide you with the driver, but in some cases, you will have to write the driver code following the datasheet or user manual of the hardware devices.

In this section, we will discuss how to connect an external IR sensor to the BeagleBoard. The IR sensor we use in this chapter is ZMotion (ZEPIR0AxS02MODG shown in the following figure) from *Zilog Co. Ltd.*, which is a double-mode IR sensor providing both the serial communication and IO interface. Therefore, we can introduce two classic external device-driving methods with a single sensor.

Firstly, let's brief the typical sensor/actuator interface. Currently, there could be more than million types of sensor/actuator equipped all over the world. But this doesn't mean that we have to know millions of interfaces. Basically, all these millions of interfaces could be classified into the following two categories:

- Analog interface
- Serial communication interface

The analog interface includes the following types:

- Voltage: Numerous sensors belong to this kind, such as tilt sensor, accelerometer sensor, humidity, and so on. The sensor output is a voltage, which could be sampled using ADC. This kind of sensor is the most common interface to be integrated into an embedded system.

- Resistor: The output is a resistor with the value changed with physical parameters, including temperature and light sensor. We usually need a voltage source to power these sensors and sample the value.

- Current: This is a popular interface in industry due to its stability, which is achieved by converting the voltage into current. With the aid of a resistor, it can be sampled following the same method as voltage output.

The serial communication interface means exchanging information bits sequentially with other devices through a communication channel (trace on the board or interface cable). The common serial interface includes UART, I2C, SPI, and some advanced serial communication protocols, such as RS422, RS485, and MODBUS. The serial communication interface is very popular in advanced sensors/actuators, since it can provide complex configuration and operation mode.

Now, let's get back to the context of this chapter. The target device is the ZMotion IR sensor, the datasheet for which can be obtained from `www.zilog.com/docs/ PS0284.pdf`. According to the datasheet, ZMotion can provide two interface modes. The simple mode based on the digital I/O interface, in which the pin 5 will be the output pin. As soon as a motion event is detected, the pin 5 will change its voltage to reflect the situation. Considering that the IR detection is an ON/OFF event, the voltage output will also follow the 0/1 fashion. Therefore, it was usually named as the digital I/O interface. In brief, the voltage on pin 5 will be equal to VDD if there is no motion detected, and will be equal to 0 if there is motion detected for a short time. Under this condition, the BeagleBoard does not need an external ADC device to obtain the voltage change event, yet a simple GPIO on the BeagleBoard will be able to capture such an event.

According to the BeagleBoard user manual, the main extension board provided 22 GPIO pins. What we need is just one of them. But here comes a new problem – which is also very general in prototype development – the voltage mismatch. The voltage level of the BeagleBoard, or in other words the GPIO pins, is 1.8V. If we check the datasheet of ZMotion, the operating voltage of interface is 3.3V. It's easy to note that they cannot fit with each other; simply connecting them will not only cause wrong data (for example, the logical 1 with 1.8V device may be treated as logical 0 with 3.3V device), but may also damage the devices. Before any software development, we will have to deal with this hardware problem first.

Voltage shifting

In detail, what we need to fix are two problems: one is how to power the ZMotion device, and the other is how to make them be able to talk to each other. There are many solutions to solve these problems; however, most of them will involve hardware assembling and require necessary electronic design experience.

Here, in this chapter, we are considering a ready-to-use solution, which is more suitable for users without an electronic background (for example, if you are from computer science). The trainer board from *Tincan Co. Ltd.* (http://www.tincantools.com/) has been designed to work with BeagleBoard-XM and includes a 1.8V to 3.3V bi-directional converting function. The selling price is only $59, which should be affordable for most users. We may also need to purchase another useful device—the breadboard—which is very helpful in rapid prototype development. A breadboard doesn't cost much, and is easily available at eBay, Amazon, or a local electronics shop.

Make sure you have the following modules in hands:

- BeagleBoard
- Trainer board
- ZMotion module
- Breadboard
- Several solderless jump cables

Now please take the following steps to connect the ZMotion module with BeagleBoard through trainer board. After these steps, you will get the hardware system ready to run as shown in the following figure:

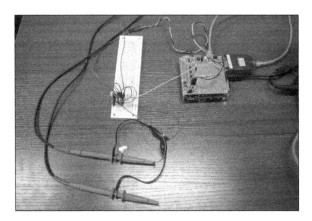

1. Attach the trainer board to the BeagleBoard:

This device is specially designed to work with the BeagleBoard, which means you can directly attach it to the BeagleBoard through the **main extension** connector. The trainer board should also be shipped with some spacers and screws to help you in fixing the two boards. The process is very simple; however, if you need detailed instructions, it can be found at `http://www.elinux.org/BeagleBoard_Trainer`.

2. Insert the ZMotion module into the breadboard:

   As shown in the previous figure, a breadboard is designed with typical space gaps. You can simply insert the ZMotion or any other devices into it. Moreover, each column of the breadboard is internally connected. Therefore, we can utilize solderless wires to connect different modules to implement a pre-defined schematic.

3. Use wires to connect different module by following this schematic:

   The trainer board will automatically connect to the BeagleBoard through a main extension connector, get power, and pass signals as shown in the following figure. Therefore, we only need to connect the breadboard and the trainer board.

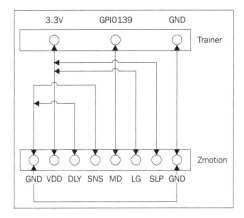

Interfacing sensors via digital I/O in Simulink

Congratulations, now the hardware system is ready to use. Let's get back to the software design. Here we will introduce the simpler approach — the Simulink method to drive the ZMotion sensor through the built-in BeagleBoard Support Package. The introduction of Simulink has been described in the previous chapter, based on which we will be able to achieve this aim quite easily.

First, let's start a new Simulink model and open the Simulink library by typing `simulink` in the command window of MATLAB. Locate **Simulink Support Package for BeagleBoard Hardware** in the Simulink library browser and click on it; you will easily see that the GPIO driver has already been provided by the **GPIO Read** and **GPIO Write** blocks. Please go through the following steps to set up a new Simulink model to drive the ZMotion module through the BeagleBoard:

1. Simply drag a **GPIO Read** block into the system model, as shown in the following screenshot. Then double click on it to configure the settings of the **GPIO Read** block. Let's set the **GPIO number** to 139 (you can use any GPIO pin you wish; just remember to connect the hardware accordingly).

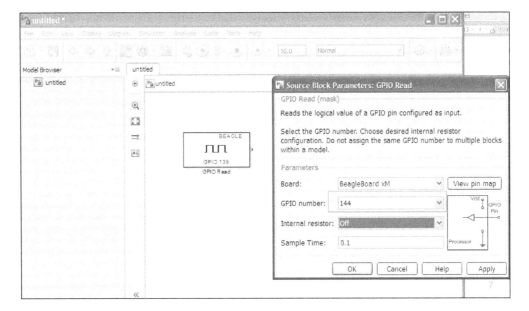

2. Drag a **Scope** block as the display for the system setup and connect a wire between the **GPIO Read** block and the **Scope** block.

3. Drag a **GPIO Write** block into the model, and set the **GPIO number** to **144**. This operation will set the direction of the voltage convertor connecting GPIO 139 on the trainer board. According to the schematic of the trainer board (http://www.elinux.org/images/6/6b/Trainer_Rev-B_schematic.pdf), a logical 1 in the GPIO 144 will set the direction from 1.8V to 3.3V, while a logical 0 in the GPIO 144 will set the direction from 3.3V to 1.8V.

4. Now let's add an **LED** control block to trigger an alarm as a sample actuator when a motion event is detected. Please set the LED to USR0.

5. To make the system output easier to monitor, we will set up a comparing output using a **Pulse Generator** block with an **LED** control block as shown in the following screenshot. Set the LED number to USR0.

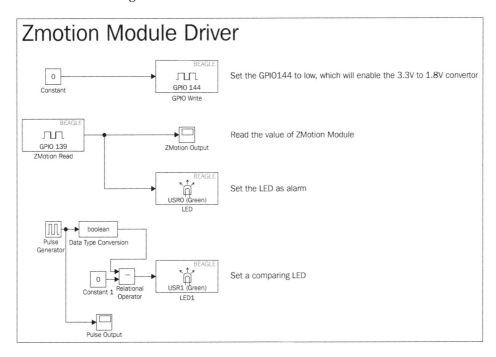

Until now, we have created a minimized system, which is ready to be implemented in the BeagleBoard. For your convenience, a ready-to-use Simulink model `ZMotion_Detect.slx` has been enclosed in the code folder.

Let's navigate to **Tools | Run on Target hardware | Prepare to Run** to set up the necessary configuration following the discussion of the previous chapter. After the configuration, we can run the application by navigating to **Tools | Run on Target hardware | Run**. We may need to wait a few seconds for the compiling and downloading process, and then you will see the **Scope** block having continuous output of logical 1. This is because there is nothing detected. So let's put the breadboard with the ZMotion module inserted at a suitable place, for example, opposite the door.

You may also want to see what the system will output, so adjust your screen to the same direction. You can now move to the front of the ZMotion module; the output of the **Scope** block in the Simulink window will change to logical 0. Try to move in and out several times; you will see the **Scope** block output window changes accordingly (as shown in the following screenshot), as well as the LED flashing in the BeagleBoard.

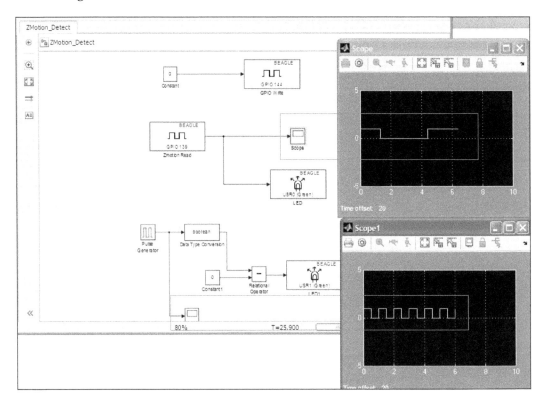

Congratulations, you have now built a simple home security application: you got the motion detect function, as well as the reacting alarm function using LED. You can extend the function of this system as you wish. You can add any Simulink modules into the system to build a much more complex algorithm, for example, the audio player block we implemented before. You may also extend its capability by integrating more sensor inputs to form an advanced system.

Interfacing sensors via a serial port in C

In the last section, the ZMotion IR sensor was connected to the BeagleBoard through the digital I/O interface, and successfully acquired the value of the ZMotion module into Simulink by using the **GPIO Write** block and the **GPIO Read** block. In this section, we will not only discuss how to connect a sensor based on a different interface (that is, serial communication) but also how to develop a software driver to communicate with the sensor. We will use the textual C code approach in this section, and you can migrate the code into a S-Function block for graphical programming in Simulink, which will be discussed later.

Firstly, let's get back to the datasheet of the ZMotion module. To select the **Serial Interface Mode**, we will need to provide a pull-up resistor (typically 100 KΩ) from TXD/SNS to VDD during the power ON process. If the device detects the voltage on that pin is greater than 2.5V in the power ON process, the device will enable the serial mode.

Secondly, there is an important issue which we have to fix in the trainer board. The trainer board uses a TXS0102 bi-directional voltage convertor for the TXD and RXD signal from the BeagleBoard. A jumper is provided, but the signals are directly connected to the MCU in the trainer board through traces at the back of the board. As a result, although we can connect the TXD and RXD signal with the matched voltage level to the ZMotion module (3.3V), the communication process will be interfered with by the MCU in the trainer board. To solve this problem, we will have to make a tiny modification to the trainer board by cutting off the traces (highlighted with red lines in the following figure) using a knife. After this treatment, you can still enable the UART communication between the BeagleBoard and trainer board MCU with jumper headers.

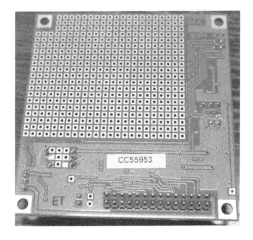

Now, we are able to connect the system similar to the I/O mode connections. The overall connection scheme has been provided in the following figure, which will require only one additional resistor.

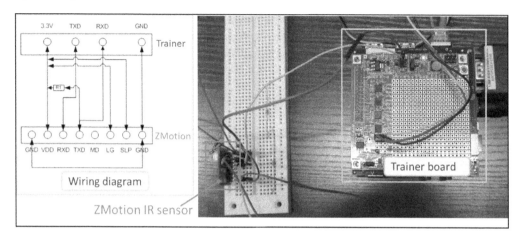

Now let's think about how to implement the driver code for the ZMotion module based on serial communication. The first step is to enable the serial port in the BeagleBoard through C code. We will start a new C project targeting the BeagleBoard in Eclipse, and name it as ZMotionSerial. The full serial function is provided by the standard C libraries fcntl.h, errno.h, signal.h, stdlib.h, termios.h, unistd.h, stdio.h, and string.h, which should be added to the source file (main.c).

Then, we will need to write some driver functions for the serial port. Usually, at least four functions should be implemented: serial_port_open(), serial_port_close(), serial_port_read(), and serial_port_write().

The serial_port_open() function is responding for the initialization, which will open the specified serial port (the serial port in the main extension interface is UART2, which is /dev/tty01). Set the baud rate (9600 for the ZMotion module) and related parameters.

```
int serial_port_open(void)
{ struct termios options;
  serial_port = open(PORT_NAME, O_RDWR | O_NONBLOCK);
  if (serial_port != -1) {
    printf("Serial Port open\n");
    tcgetattr(serial_port,&options_original);
    tcgetattr(serial_port, &options);
    cfmakeraw(&options);
```

```
      cfsetispeed(&options, B9600);
      cfsetospeed(&options, B9600);
      if (tcsetattr(serial_port, TCSANOW, &options)!=0) {
        printf("error %d from tcsetattr", errno);
        return (-1);
      }
    }
    else {
      printf("Unable to open %s",PORT_NAME);
      printf("Error %d opening %s: %s",errno, PORT_NAME,
        strerror(errno));
    }
    return (serial_port);
  }
```

The `serial_port_close()` function is the inverse of the open function, which will disable the serial port before closing the application.

```
  void serial_port_close()
  { tcsetattr(serial_port,TCSANOW,&options_original);
    close(serial_port);
  }
```

The most important functions are the `serial_port_read()` and `serial_port_write()` function, which will be frequently called to implement the driver of ZMotion.

```
  int serial_port_read(char *read_buffer, size_t max_chars_to_read)
  { int chars_read = read(serial_port, read_buffer,
      max_chars_to_read);
    return chars_read;
  }
  void serial_port_write(char write_buffer)
  { int bytes_written;
    size_t len = 0;
    len = 1;
    bytes_written = write(serial_port, &write_buffer, len);
    if (bytes_written < len)
      printf("Write failed \n");
  }
```

The `serial_port_write()` function will write a char into the serial port, while the `serial_port_read()` function will try to read up to `max_chars_to_read` bytes of data from the serial port if there are any.

The next step is how to communicate with the ZMotion module with these functions. If we check the ZMotion datasheet, especially the Serial Interface Mode section, the ZMotion module was designed with a very simple serial communication protocol. As shown in the following figure, the host device (that is, the BeagleBoard) first sends a command to the ZMotion module, and then the ZMotion module will response with a result as shown in the following figure:

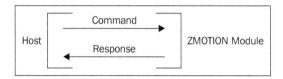

In this simple example, we will implement the basic command a, which is a read-motion-status command. The response could be **Y**, **N**, or **U**. **Y** means there is motion detected, **N** means there is no motion detected, and **U** means the ZMotion module is not ready for use. It's easy to notice that this command exactly replaces the function of the OUTPUT pin in the digital I/O interface. A Check_ZMotion_Status() function has been implemented.

```
int Check_ZMotion_Status()
{
  char read_buffer[MAX_COMMAND_LENGTH + 1] = {0};
  char *pRead;
  int chars_read;

  serial_port_write(0x61);
  usleep(12000);
  chars_read = serial_port_read(read_buffer,MAX_COMMAND_LENGTH);
  pRead = read_buffer;
  while (chars_read > 0)
  {
    if(*pRead=='Y') {
      printf("Y \n");
      return 1;
    }
    else if(*pRead=='N') {
      printf("N \n");
    }
    else if(*pRead=='U') {
      printf("U \n");
    }
    else {
```

```
        printf("Wrong response. \n");
    }
    chars_read--;
    pRead++;
  }
  return 0;
}
```

One thing that we should pay attention to is the time gap between command and response, because of which we insert a `usleep(12000)` function to force the program to wait 12 ms before trying to read the response. Generally, you can read the response later, since there is a buffer implemented in the lower layer of Linux. But you will get a NULL return if you read it earlier. The 12 ms delay is contributed by the ZMotion process time and the Linux process time.

In the `main()` function, we only need to call the `Check_ZMotion_Status()` function regularly to carry out the motion-detecting task.

```
// The main program loop:
for (;;)
{ // The application can perform other tasks here.
  Check_ZMotion_Status();
}
```

We can now build the project to get the executable for the BeagleBoard, and issue it from the command line through PuTTY as we did in the previous chapters. Similar to the Simulink approach, please adjust the ZMotion module and your screen, move around, and check the output of this program.

The ZMotion module provides tens of commands with different purposes, which can be simply implemented in C code following a similar approach. The combination of these commands can achieve a more complex ZMotion operation mode.

MATLAB-based algorithm integration

We can benefit from the rapid prototype approach in C code as well. After we make the serial driver ready, it can be easily integrated with the algorithm written in MATLAB. Recall what we have done in the previous chapter: the complex algorithm can be quickly implemented in high-level MATLAB m-script and then compiled into a static C library. In the `main()` function (refer to `main_avg.c` file in the source code of *Chapter 5*), we can call both the device driver and the algorithm function. In this section, we will provide a simple example, which will utilize the MATLAB algorithm that we developed in the previous chapter.

The algorithm is based on the fact that there could be a "false alarm". A false alarm means the device gives out the positive signal, but there is no such motion in the real world. The false alarm is due to the noise inside the device and the environment, especially when the device is switched into high-sensitivity mode. Therefore, we usually need to deploy an algorithm to filter the false alarm. The simplest filtering algorithm is to read the sensor several times and then calculate the average value of the readings. For changing the operation mode of the ZMotion module, we need two more functions, `Enable_HyperSense(int type)` and `Set_Sensetivity(int value)`, to enable and set the ZMotion module into high-sensitivity mode, respectively. By following ZMotion's operation manual, the implementation of these two functions is straightforward. Please refer to the source code in the main files (for example, `main_avg.c`) for more details.

The main loop in the `main()` function looks as follows:

```
for (;;)
{
  // The application can perform other tasks here.
  temp = Check_ZMotion_Status();
  if(temp == 1)//Motion detected
  {// to reduce false alarms, get 5 consecutive IR
    // readings in hyper sense mode and computer the mean
    Enable_HyperSense(1);//enable the hyper sense mode
    Set_Sensetivity(1);//set high sensitivity mode
    for (i=1;i<5;i++)
    {
      temp = Check_ZMotion_Status();
      x[i]=temp;
      usleep(100000);
    }
    //call MATLAB function calcavg() to get average
    if (calcavg2(x)>0.5) // make a decision
      decision=1;
    else
      decision=0;
    printf("IR detect decision=%d\n",decision);
    Enable_HyperSense(0);//disable hyper sense mode
    Set_Sensetivity(128);//set normal sensitivity
  }
  usleep(100000);
}
```

In the previous code, variable x is an array of double type defined by double x[5] at the beginning of the main function. In the loop, the procedure is changed slightly to reduce false alarms. By default, the IR sensor works at normal sense mode, and once the device detects a motion event, it will switch into the algorithm of reducing false alarms. The algorithm will take five readings with high sensitivity from the ZMotion module and pass them to the MATLAB function calcavg2() that will calculate the mean value of these five readings. The mean value is compared against a threshold of 0.5 to decide if a motion is detected. The result is displayed as shown in the following screenshot. Then switch the system into normal sense mode and back to the loop.

The data processing function calcavg2() is the same as function calcavg() in the previous chapter, except it takes five double numbers instead of 10 numbers for average calculation. For more details, please see calcavg2.m under the calcav2 folder in this chapter's source code folder.

In order to let the MATLAB Coder know that the input of `calcavg2()` is five double numbers, we need to change the type of the input argument to `double(1x5)` in the MATLAB Coder project `calcavg2.prj`. Another way, with more flexibility, is to specify that the size of the input argument is variable-size with fixed upper bounds.

It is worth remembering that in order to include the C code generated from MATLAB, we need to set up a link folder in our Eclipse project. Please refer to the previous chapter for more details.

Try to build and issue the new project for the BeagleBoard (the ready-to-use C file of `ZMotionSerial` has been provided as well). In this case, you'd better move towards the system and compare with another moving pattern. A few sample results have been provided in the previous screenshot.

Other things to try

So far, we have developed the serial communication driver in C and built an IR motion detection application. In order to improve the performance (that is, reduce false alarms), we made use of the advanced feature of the IR sensor and integrated a data-processing algorithm developed in MATLAB into the application.

If you prefer a Simulink development environment, you can follow the section *Writing a Simulink device driver block for BeagleBoard* discussed in the previous chapter to integrate these C driver code into a Simulink S-Function block for graphical programming. As a result, you will get a serial communication driver block for BeagleBoard in Simulink.

As you can see in the filtering algorithm for reducing false alarms, we have to wait for five readings and then calculate their average in a batch off-line mode. For a better computation efficiency and shorter response time, the algorithm can be improved by using a **moving average filter** that calculates the mean in a recursive fashion. For demonstration, a **Simple Moving Average (SMA)** filter has been developed in m-script file `IR_sma.m` and the main file has also been modified a bit accordingly. These two files, namely `IR_sma.m` and `main_sma.c`, can be found in this chapter's source code folder.

The SMA algorithm can be explained by a mathematical equation:

$$\bar{x}_{new} = \bar{x}_{last} + (x_k - x_{k-5})/5$$

where x_k is the present readings at time k, $\bar{x}_{new}$ is the new average to be determined, and $\bar{x}_{last}$ is the last average. The SMA is implemented in `IR_sma.m` by the following code:

```
data_pre5=data_vector(1); % take the oldest data
data_vector=[data_vector(2:5) input]; % shift the data
avg=avg_pre+(input-data_pre5)/5; % calculate average recursively
avg_pre=avg;
```

Some key points of `IR_sma.m` are as follows:

- A persistent variable `data_vector` is defined to store previous readings. `data_vector` works like a queue, and each time `IR_sma.m` is called, we shift the data in `data_vector` to remove the oldest reading and pad the latest reading into `data_vector`.

- The input argument, namely `input`, is only one reading instead of a vector of all of the last 10 readings. As a result, the response time will be only one reading period, rather than a waiting time for 10 readings. Each time when a new IR reading is available, `IR_sma.m` is called to determine the average of the last five readings and a decision is made.

Summary

In this chapter, we have implemented the driver for a ZMotion IR sensor using two different methods, digital I/O in graphical Simulink and serial communication in textual C code, for setting up a simple home security application. We also demonstrated how to integrate with a data processing algorithm generated from MATLAB.

Following from this point, you will have the ability to build most sensor-based applications, write code to drive them, and utilize the convenient algorithm development based on the rapid prototype idea. In the next chapter, we will look into more complex applications: the multimedia for rapid prototyping.

6
Voice Recognition

Audio and speech processing systems have become very common in the everyday lives of people, from film studios and portable music players to **Voice over Internet Protocol (VoIP)** systems such as Skype. In this chapter, we look at how to use speech processing techniques and MATLAB/Simulink rapid prototyping to build a voice recognition system.

This chapter begins with an overview of digital audio signals before considering signal processing. Then we look at the general structure and workflow of voice recognition systems, which contains usually two parts: training and recognition. A section on feature extraction covers the audio feature extraction techniques, followed by a section on the training procedure and pattern analysis. The last section on recognition demonstrates the voice recognition system that determines which voice command the utterance of an unknown input voice is.

This chapter will cover the following topics in a step-by-step manner:

- Setting up and connecting the hardware of the voice recognition system
- Development of voice recognition systems in three steps: feature extraction, pattern analysis for training, and pattern matching for recognition
- Performance optimization by tuning parameters on the fly

By the end of this chapter, we will have a voice recognition system that controls the LED. The demos in this chapter are good starting points for developing and prototyping a more advanced voice recognition system.

Defining the voice recognition task

Voice recognition is the process of determining the identity of speakers and/or what the speakers say in their voices.

> *A full definition is given by Russ Adams as "the technology by which sounds, words or phrases spoken by humans are converted into electrical signals, and these signals are transformed into coding patterns to which meaning has been assigned" [Adams1990].*

Voice recognition is related to, and overlaps with, two very similar applications: speaker recognition and speech recognition. Speaker recognition is the automated determination of who is speaking, and speech recognition is to determine what is being said. In addition, there is a difference between the act of authentication (commonly referred to as speaker verification) and identification. Another way to differentiate between voice recognition systems is by determining if they can handle only discrete words, connected words, or continuous speech.

In this chapter, our voice recognition task is to verify which voice command the speaker is saying and then take actions accordingly. More specifically, there are two voice commands: ON and OFF. When the speaker says "ON" (or a specific word, for example, Daniel), the voice recognition program turns the LED ON. When a voice of "OFF" (or another word, for example, Linda) is detected, the LED is turned OFF.

The voice recognition example presented in this chapter is designed for a single speaker. It can be applied to multiple speakers or speaker-independent applications straightway without changes, but recognition performance may be sacrificed.

Voice recognition covers a wide field and could be a very complicated procedure. This chapter is intended to provide you with the basics of prototyping a speech recognition application. We consider primarily the case of discrete word recognizers, as this is a lower-level but fundamental recognition task of any advanced voice recognition system.

Configuration of the voice recognition system

In this chapter, for the purpose of demonstration, we use the output of the recognition system to control the LED on the BeagleBoard. If the BeagleBoard with voice recognition capability is connected with external actuators and peripheral devices, it can be used to turn on and turn off TV, voice authorization, and so on.

The following figure illustrates the configuration of the voice recognition example and some additional devices and packages required for this example:

- Hardware: A microphone with a 3.5 mm jack
- Software: The DSP system toolbox in MATLAB/Simulink

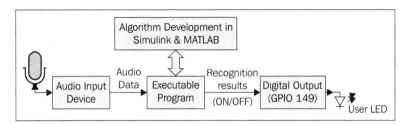

As shown in the previous figure, the microphone is connected to the BeagleBoard's audio-in port and the sound is converted into sampled digital audio data by the audio input device (an accelerated audio encoding and decoding (CODEC) chip TPS65950) on the BeagleBoard. The digital audio data is a stream of 16-bit integers sampling at a specified rate. The audio data is presented in the form of a matrix in MATLAB and a frame in a Simulink. The data processing algorithm is developed in Simulink and MATLAB environment and downloaded onto the BeagleBoard as an executable program. The executable takes the audio data as its input and sends the recognition results. Here, the recognition result is a logic value 1 for ON and 0 for OFF. The logic value is used to control the BeagleBoard's user LED through the BeagleBoard's **General Purpose Input/Output (GPIO)** 149. From the view of software development, the digital output is done by a Simulink block called **GPIO Write**.

Digital audio signals

In most applications, analog sound is first sampled and converted into an integer at some sampling rate. With respect to the BeagleBoard, the conversion of analog sound into a digital audio signal is done by the TPS65950 chip. The two most important characters in digital audio are sampling rate and resolution. The sampling rate specifies how fast the sound is sampled, and resolution is defined as how many bits are used for representing one sample. The sound can be completely specified by the sequence of these integer numbers and the sample rate. The following table lists these characters in some common audio systems:

Application	Sample rate	Resolution	Note
Telephone	8 kHz	8-12 bits	

Application	Sample rate	Resolution	Note
Mobile phone	8 kHz	14-16 bits	GSM
Portable music player	32 kHz	14-16 bits	MP3, WMA
CD audio	44.1 kHz	16 bits	Stored on CD

Handling audio in MATLAB/Simulink

In general, the sampled audio data are saved as a file in computer systems. For example, a `*.wav` file may save the digital audio data at 16-bit resolution and 44.1 kHz sampling rate.

For processing audio data in MATLAB and Simulink, the sampled audio is usually stored as a vector of samples, with each individual value being a double-precision floating point number. Any operation that MATLAB can perform on a vector, in theory, can be performed on stored audio as well. The audio vector can be loaded and saved in the same way as any other MATLAB variable—processed, added, plotted, and so on.

Frame-based signal processing in Simulink

The Simulink support package for BeagleBoard has provided a function block to capture the sound and automatically generate the executables, only after which we can work with digital audio processing, without being too concerned with how the sound is captured. In this chapter, we will confine our discussions primarily to the voice recognition algorithm and how to implement the algorithm through MATLAB and Simulink rapid prototyping.

Simulink supports both sample-based and frame-based signal processing. The sample-based signal in Simulink is a stream of samples. Sampled-signals are the easiest to construct by sampling a real-world (physical) signal at a given sample rate and, in general, most digital-to-analog converters output sample-based signals. In Simulink, a single line between two blocks represents a sample-based signal and Simulink blocks in sample-based operations process signals one sample at a time.

As frame-based signal processing has the benefits of reduced overhead and improved throughput, most real-time **digital signal processing (DSP)** systems optimize throughput rates by processing data in **batch** or **frame-based** mode. Each frame is a collection of consecutive signal samples that have been buffered into a single container and organized in the form of matrices. Thus a frame has several columns and each column represents consecutive samples of one input signal. For example, as shown in the following figure, the output of the BeagleBoard's **ALSA Audio Capture** block is a frame signal with size n-by-2. Here, the two columns represent the samples of two audio channels. n is referred to as frame size in this block's configuration window and indicates how many samples of each channel are in one frame. In the following figure, the BeagleBoard's output ALSA Audio Capture block is a 2205-by-2 frame. Given the sampling rate of 22050 Hz, one such frame is generated at every 0.1 s and the so-called frame rate is 10 frames per second. The concept of frame-based signal processing is illustrated in the following figure:

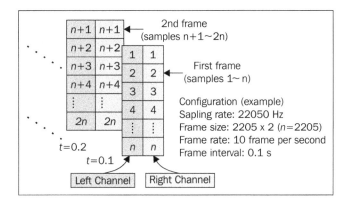

A double line between two blocks indicates that we are using frames and the blocks carry out frame-based processing. To view the frame sizes of frame-based signals, you can navigate to **Format | Port/Signal Displays | Signal Dimensions**. To view the frame rate (how many frames are processed in very second), navigate to **Format | Sample Time Display | Colors** which shows the frame rate of different colors.

By propagating these multisample frames instead of the individual signal, the overhead of data transmission among blocks is significantly reduced. As a result, a completely frame-based Simulink model can run several times faster than the same model processing sample-by-sample in both simulation and code generation.

Structure of a voice recognition system

Although voice recognition systems differ in various ways, many of them, if not all, require some form of training which acclimatizes the system. Voice recognition systems usually share some common and fundamental techniques and have a similar structure as shown in the following figure:

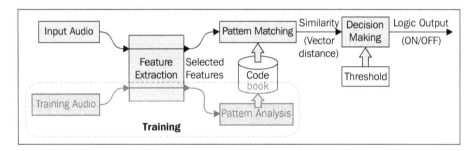

A voice recognition system usually consists of three function blocks:

- Feature extraction
- Pattern analysis (for training)
- Pattern matching (for recognition)

The workflow of a voice recognition system can be divided into two sessions:

- Training
- Recognition

Feature extraction is a process of transforming the large number of audio samples into a relatively small set of discriminatory features. The features are carefully chosen so that the features set are expected to be a good representation of the voice, without using the whole and large amount of audio data samples. **Pattern analysis** is to find the distribution of these features and their relationship with the meanings of the voice. The resulting distribution of features is usually presented as a reference model (or referred to as **codebook**). Pattern analysis is the core of the training process with the purpose of building a codebook that is used in pattern matching.

Since each person's voice is different, the voice recognition program must be first trained with a user's voice input to get used to it before that user's voice can be recognized by the program. During a training session, the program carries out the feature extraction and learns the pattern of the user's voice. The pattern associated to a spoken word is referred to as the codebook of the word. When a training session is finished, a codebook is generated to store these patterns and their associated meanings. In practice, such a priori information of a user's voice is usually captured when candidate users are registered with the system, and would be available in a real system.

In **pattern matching**, the program attempts to match the features of an input voice with a pattern that is acquired in the training session. Pattern matching is usually implemented by calculating the similarity between the features of an input voice and the pattern of a known voice. The purpose of comparison is to find the best pattern that matches with the extracted features of input voices to the greatest extent. In other words, its purpose is to find the pattern that has the highest similarity with the input voice.

In the recognition session, the features of the input voice are first extracted in the same way as feature extraction in the training session. Then the pattern-matching procedure follows, where the extracted features are compared against the existing patterns in the codebook and their similarities are calculated. Once the best pattern that matches the input voice is found, the meaning of the voice is said to be recognized, which finishes the task of voice recognition.

Sometimes, a decision-making block is used to reduce the false rate of voice recognition and enhance its robustness. A simple decision-making method is the threshold approach, which compares the similarity given by pattern matching against a pre-defined threshold. If the similarity score is higher than the threshold, the pattern matching is regarded as valid and we have high confidence in the recognition result. If the similarity score is too low, the likelihood of successful recognition is less and it would be safe to reject the recognition results.

This chapter is intended to provide you with the basics of prototyping a speech recognition application. For the sake of discussion, we have two separate Simulink models for training and recognition, respectively.

Feature extraction

We first look at feature extraction, which is a common block shared by both pattern analysis for training and pattern matching for recognition.

Various kinds of audio features have been proposed for voice recognition, including **linear predictive coding (LPC)**, cepstral coefficients, spectral coefficients, and so on. The **Mel-Frequency Cepstral Coefficients (MFCC)** are probably the most popular at present due to their simplicity and pretty good performance. In this chapter, we are using the MFCC features and associated feature-extraction techniques to build a demonstrative system, as we focus on the demonstration of rapid prototyping. Obviously, a voice recognition system may use a combination of different kinds of features for better recognition performance.

MFCC is based on the fact that the human perception system has a non-linear frequency response to sounds. The frequency response of human's ear works like a band of filters spaced linearly at low frequencies and logarithmically at high frequencies used to capture the important characteristics of speech. Therefore, for each tone at a frequency of f Hz, a subjective pitch is measured on a scale called the **Mel scale**. The Mel scale is linear frequency spacing below 1000 Hz and a logarithmic spacing above 1000 Hz.

The MFCC are the coefficients of cosine transform of the real logarithm of the short-term energy spectrum expressed on a Mel-frequency scale. The main purpose of the MFCC calculation is to mimic the behavior of human ears. The MFCC feature-extraction steps are shown in the following figure and implemented in the MATLAB function `mfcc.m` in this chapter:

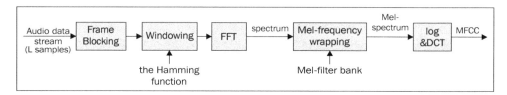

The block diagram of MFCC feature extraction and the code of `mfcc.m` are explained as follows:

1. **Frame Blocking**: The motivation for frame blocking is the quasi-stationary nature of speech, as human speech is usually segmented into small sections of 20 to 30 ms. These sections are called frames. Thus, the continuous audio stream is divided into frames and each frame contains n samples. In order to avoid loss of information, an overlap of 1/3~1/2 of the frame size n is used between adjacent frames. Usually the frame size is equal to power of two in order to facilitate the use of FFT. We use typical values for frame size n and overlap m of n=256 and m=100.

Frame blocking is implemented in MATLAB script as follows:

```
n = 256; % n: frame size
m = 100; % m: overlap
lenSig = length(u); % length of input signal u
nbFrame = floor((lenSig - n) / m) + 1; % number of possible
  frames
framedSig=zeros(n,nbFrame);
for i = 1:n
  for j = 1:nbFrame
    framedSig(i, j) = u(((j - 1) * m) + i);
  end
end
```

Here, `nbFrame` is the number of possible frames for an audio signal `u` with length `lenSig`. The output is `frameSig`, a 256-by-nbFrame matrix, where the column vectors of `frameSig` are the frames of audio data.

2. **Window weighting**: For each frame, a window-weighting function is applied to increase the continuity between adjacent frames. Common weighting functions include the rectangular window, the **Hamming window**, the Blackman window, and the flattop window. In this example, the most commonly used Hamming window function is used and each frame is multiplied by the Hamming window function:

```
h = hamming(n);
framedSig2 = diag(h) * framedSig1;
```

We then create a new matrix `frameSig2` with each column being an audio data frame weighted by the Hamming function.

3. **Fast Fourier Transform (FFT) and power spectrum**: An FFT is used to get the spectrum information. Applying an FFT to each column of `framedSig2` and computing magnitudes of the FFT coefficients, we create a new matrix `framedFFT`.

```
framedFFT=zeros(size(framedSig2));
for i = 1:nbFrame
  framedFFT(:,i) = abs(fft(framedSig2(:, i)));
end
```

Each column of `framedFFT` is a power-spectrum representation of the audio signal. The power spectrum indicates which frequency band the voice energy is concentrated in.

4. **Mel scale spectrum by Mel-frequency wrapping**: The magnitude spectrum is then transformed into the Mel scale. This transform is usually called **Mel-frequency wrapping** and is performed using a bank of Mel-filters spacing on the Mel scale. Each Mel-filter is a bandpass filter with triangular-shape frequency response at desired frequency range. To mimic the frequency response of human ears, these filters are linearly distributed for low frequencies (below 1 kHz) and logarithmically at higher frequencies. In our MATLAB script, this is implemented by a subfunction `melfb()` in `melfspectrum.m`.

```
function z = melfspectrum (nMelf, nFFT, fs, data) %#codegen
```

Function `melfspectrum()` has four input arguments:

- ° `nMelf`: This is the number of Mel-filters in the filter bank
- ° `nFFT`: This the length of the FFT
- ° `fs`: This the sample rate in Hz
- ° `data`: These are the frames of the power spectrum

The return value `z` is an `nMelf`-by-`nbFrame` matrix, each column of which represents the power spectrum in Mel-scale. The number of Mel-filters is chosen between 12 and 20, since most of the voice signal information is represented at a low frequency (alternatively, at the first few Mel-filters).

5. **MFCC**: The last stage of the MFCC computation involves performing a **discrete cosine transform** (**DCT**) on the log of the Mel-spectrum. This is done by:

```
z = melfspectrum (16, n, fs, framedFFT);
v = dct(log(z));
```

The DCT is for transforming information from Mel-frequency to the time domain.

As a result of MFCC feature extraction, the large size n-by-m audio data frame (for example, 256 x 141 for 1 s voice at 22.05 kHz sampling rate) is transformed into a small size `nMelf`-by-`nbFrame` (for example, 16 x 141) of features.

Training session

In the training session, we are collecting the voices of ON and OFF which are used to develop the codebook for recognition. The audio captured from the microphone connected to the BeagleBoard is saved to the MATLAB workspace for pattern analysis and pattern code generation.

Voice acquisition and segmentation

As shown in the following screenshot, a Simulink model `VocRcgBB_Trn.mdl` has been developed for training and creating the code book. The ALSA Audio Capture block is configured to a sampling frequency of 22050 Hz and sends out the stereo audio data in a 2205 x 2 frame of 16-bit integers at interval 0.1 s. For floating point processing, the **Normalize** block converts the captured two-channel audio data (a 2205 x 2 integer matrix) into single-channel double data (a 2205 x 1 double vector).

The rest of the model consists of the following function blocks:

1. The buffer block (highlighted by a red circle numbered 1) is configured to buffer size 22050 and buffer overlap 9*2205. This makes the output of the buffer block a frame of 1-second audio data, which are used as training data depending on whether a valid voice is detected.

2. The group of four blocks (**RMS**, **Unbuffer**, **Hit Crossing**, and **Delay**) work as voice detection and segmentation. For each frame, the power of the voice is calculated by the RMS block. Then the Hit Crossing block checks if the signal is loud enough to be a valid voice. If the signal's power is too small, the signal could be a background noise or an invalid voice. Once a valid voice is detected, a rising pulse is generated, which triggers the **Training subsystem** after a delay of eight frames. The purpose of using eight-frame delay is to allow the **Training subsystem** to acquire two frames before the voice detection and eight frames after the voice detection..

3. The **Training subsystem** is a triggered system with a voice-detection pulse to trigger its execution. When the voice is loud enough, the subsystem saves the last one second of audio data into the workspace for training.

4. Depending on the selection of 0 (OFF) or 1 (ON), the audio data is saved into two variables, `trsON` and `trsOFF`, respectively, as shown in the following screenshot:

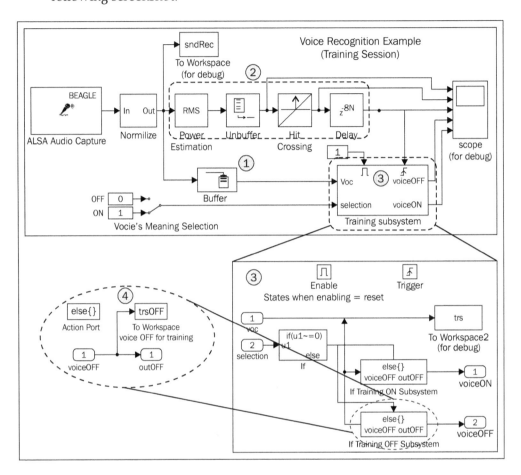

We can now run the model `VocRcgBB_Trn.mdl` to acquire the training signals. When the model starts running on the BeagleBoard, click on the switch (named **Voice Meaning Selection**) to make it 0 and speak the word "OFF" clearly. Then click on the switch to make it 1 and speak the word ON. We then get two training signals for ON and OFF, respectively.

The training signals are saved to the workspace as two variables: `trsON` and `trsOFF`. Next we perform pattern analysis to generate the codebook.

Vector Quantization (VQ) training

The extracted features are usually distributed over a high-dimensional space and different verbal words usually have different feature distribution. A voice recognition system makes use of the probability distributions of the computed feature vectors to recognize different voices. Storing every single vector generated from the training voice to represent the distribution is impossible due to the huge amount of data and low computation efficiency. The extracted features have to be analyzed to find the distribution pattern behind these vectors.

It is often easier to start by dividing the large number of feature vectors into a relatively small number of groups according to their similarities. Each group represents a region in the vector space and the feature's distribution can then be represented by a small number of regions where most vectors fall. Each region is called a cluster. A cluster can be represented by its center, called a **codeword**. The collection of all codewords for a voice is called a codebook of the voice.

Many methods have been proposed for training and pattern analysis, including **Dynamic Time Warping (DTW)**, **Hidden Markov Modeling (HMM)**, and **Vector Quantization (VQ)**. In this project, the VQ approach is used due to its ease of implementation and pretty-good performance.

The training process in the VQ approach is a clustering procedure, where these training-feature vectors are clustered to form a codebook for each training word. As a common practice in clustering, we use the well-known **Linde-Buzo-Gray (LBG)** algorithm to find the centers of clusters (in other words, the codewords of the codebook). This is implemented as a function `vqlbg()` in the MATLAB script `vqlbg.m`.

```
function codebk = vqlbg(d,k) %codegen
```

where the input argument `d` is a matrix containing training-feature vectors (one per column) and `k` is the number of clusters. The output value `codebk` is a matrix containing the codebook for training data `d`.

The LBG algorithm is a recursive procedure that generates a codebook of k codewords in stages. Mathematically, a codeword is represented by a vector and a codebook by a matrix with each column as a codeword. LBG starts first by selecting an initial codeword. In our example, it starts with using the mean of all MFCC features as the first codeword, `r=mean(d, 2)`. Then a splitting technique (that is, `r = [r*(1+e), r*(1-e)]`, where e is a small number) is used to generate two codewords. Then a nearest-neighbor search is carried out to find the nearest codeword for each training vector.

Thus, the training vectors are divided into two clusters and each codeword is updated by the mean of its associated cluster. This is implemented by `r(:, j) = mean(d(:, find(ind == j)), 2);`. The codeword-updating process is repeated until the average distance falls below the preset threshold e. Then the splitting process continues until the desired *k*-vector codebook is obtained.

As a result, the LBG training procedure divides a large set of MFCC feature vectors into a relatively small group of codewords. The set of codewords is the pattern of the voice, which represent the voice's features.

When both the training voices for ON and OFF have been acquired by running the model `VocRcgBB_Trn.mdl`, the training signals are saved as `trsOFF` and `trsON` in the MATLAB workspace. We then simply type the following two commands in the MATLAB command window to have `vqlbg()` create the codebook for each training voice:

```
codebkOFF=vqlbg(mfcc(trsOFF), 16);
codebkON=vqlbg(mfcc(trsON), 16);
```

In the recognition session, the MFCC features of the acquired voice from the speaker are compared against the codebook `codebkOFF` and `codebkON` to decide what the speaker says. Once a valid voice is recognized, corresponding action is taken.

Recognition session

The core task in a recognition session is related to the so-called pattern matching. In our case, patterns are the codebooks derived from the training voices and each pattern is linked to a class with a specific meaning, ON or OFF. The goal of pattern matching is to classify the new input voice of interest into one of these two classes. Our recognition session is to match the MFCC features of the new input voice to one of the existing codebooks.

The voice recognition is implemented in a Simulink model `VocRcgBB_Rcg.mdl`, as shown in the following screenshot:

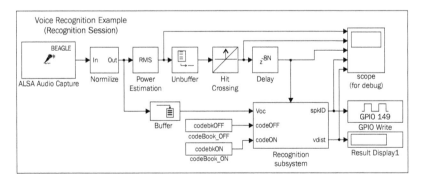

Similar to the Simulink model for training, the voice recognition model has the same pre-processing blocks, including data normalization, voice detection, and segmentation. The difference is that the **Training subsystem** is replaced by the **Recognition subsystem** and a new GPIO Write block is used to control the user LED.

The **Recognition subsystem** takes three inputs:

- 1 second buffered audio data
- codebkOFF for voice command OFF
- codebkON for OFF

codebkOFF and codebkON are two codebook matrices derived in the training session and saved in the MATLAB workspace.

The outputs of the **Recognition subsystem** are:

- spkID to indicate which voice command is identified. It has two possible values: 1 for command ON and 0 for command OFF. spkID is connected to the GPIO Write block, which interfaces with the GPIO 149 pin and controls the user LED at the BeagleBoard.
- vdmin is the minimum vector distance from the MFCC features of an unknown voice to the recognized codebook. vdmin is useful when we need to investigate the performance of voice recognition and optimize parameters.

The implementation of **Recognition Subsystem** is shown in the following screenshot:

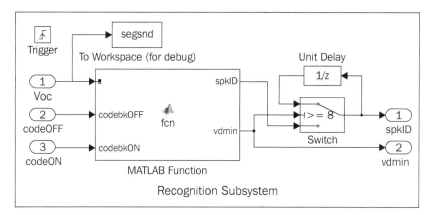

As we discussed earlier, the voice recognition task has three basic steps: feature extraction, pattern matching, and decision making. The **Recognition Subsystem** has a **MATLAB Function** block that completes the feature extraction and pattern matching. A conditional switch is used for threshold-based decision making.

The core of the **MATLAB Function** block is a MATLAB function myVocRcg.m that extracts MFCC features of the input signal u, and matches its MFCCs to codebooks (codebkON and codebkOFF).

Let us have a look at the code of function myVocRcg():

```
function [y1,y2,y3] = myVocRcg(u,codebkOFF, codebkON) %#codegen
%% variable declaration for code generation
fs=22050;
distmin = inf;
spkID = int16(-1);
d=0;
vecdist1=0;
vecdist2=0;


%% Feature extraction
% Step 1: Frame-blocking
m = 100;
n = 256;
lenSig = length(u);
nbFrame = floor((lenSig - n) / m) + 1;
framedSig=zeros(n,nbFrame);
for i = 1:n
  for j = 1:nbFrame
    framedSig(i, j) = u(((j - 1) * m) + i);
  end
end


% Step 2. Hamming Windowing
h = hamming(n);
framedSig2 = diag(h) * framedSig;


% Step 3. FFT power spectrum for each column
framedFFT=zeros(size(framedSig2));
for i = 1:nbFrame
  framedFFT(:,i) = abs(fft(framedSig2(:, i)));
end


% Step 3. Mel-frequency wrapping
z2 = melfspectrum(16, n, fs, framedFFT);


% Step 4. Compute MFCCs
v = dct(log(z2));
```

```
%% Pattern matching
% compare with the trained codebook
% for each trained voice code, compute distance
% compare against OFF (codeSpkOFF)
d = disteu(v, codebkOFF);
vecdist1 = sum(min(d,[],2)) / size(d,1);
if vecdist1 < distmin
  distmin = vecdist1;
  spkID = int16(0);
end

% compare against 'ON' (codeSpkON)
d = disteu(v, codebkON);
vecdist2 = sum(min(d,[],2)) / size(d,1);
if vecdist2 < distmin
  distmin = vecdist2;
  spkID = int16(1);
end
%% return values
y1= spkID;
y2= distmin;
y3= [vecdist1 vecdist2];
```

The first part of myVocRcg() is variable declaration, where the variable's type and size are declared for the purpose of code generation.

The second part of myVocRcg() is MFCC feature extraction, which is the same as the function mfcc() that is used in the training session. The resulting matrix v stores the extracted MFCC features of the audio signal u.

The third part of myVocRcg() is pattern matching, where the MFCC feature v is compared against both codebooks codebkON and codebkOFF to find which codebook the MFCC features of an unknown voice are the closest to.

In the VQ approach, the distance from an MFCC feature vector to the codeword of a codebook is used to measure how close the feature vectors are to the codeword. In the recognition session, the MFCC features of an unknown input voice are vector quantized using each trained codebook, and the total distance from the MFCC features to the codebook is computed. The word corresponding to the VQ codebook with the smallest total distance is identified as the meaning of the input utterance. Various distance measures can be used. In our example, the Euclidean distance is used, which is implemented in the MATLAB function disteu.m.

Two variables, namely `vecdist1` and `vecdist2`, representing the total distances from MFCC features of the unknown input voice to the codebooks `codebkON` and `codebkOFF`, respectively, are computed and the recognition result, `spkID`, is assigned to either 0 (OFF) or 1 (ON) according the smallest total distance. This finishes the pattern-matching process.

In order to increase the robustness of voice recognition against background noise and unexpected voices, the recognition result is filtered by a threshold-based decision-making process. It works on the basic principle that the smaller the distance, the more likely the correct recognition is. The decision making is implemented by a conditional switch. When the minimum total distance `vdmin` is greater than the threshold (in this example, 8), it looks more likely that the captured voice may be an unexpected voice or an impulse noise. In order to avoid a false recognition, the present recognition result should be ignored by keeping the previous result. Only when `vdmin` is less than the threshold is it safe to declare a valid voice is identified and the recognition is valid.

Running the voice recognition application

Since the voice recognition application consists of two phases, training and recognition, running the recognition application is a two-step procedure and is carried out as follows:

1. Open the training model `VocRcgBB_Trn.mdl` and run the model.

2. As `VocRcgBB_Trn.mdl` is running on the BeagleBoard, click on the **Voice Meaning Selection** switch to select which command (ON/OFF) the training voice is for. Then speak in the microphone to capture the training voice. At least one training voice for each command should be recorded.

3. When you finish, stop and close the training model. Two new variables, `trsOFF` and `codebkOFF`, should appear in the MATLAB workspace.

4. Enter the following two commands in the MATLAB command window to generate codebooks for the voice commands ON and OFF, respectively:

   ```
   codebkOFF=vqlbg(mfcc(trsOFF), 16);

   codebkON=vqlbg(mfcc(trsON), 16);
   ```

5. Open the recognition model `VocRcgBB_Rcg.mdl` and run it on the BeagleBoard. You can now speak the voice commands to control the LED. The LED is turned on and off according to your voice command.

Performance optimization by parameter tuning

In practice, for the best recognition performance, the recognition program has to be optimized for environment and configurations. For example, the background noise levels are different in different application scenarios. Different microphones have varying voice capture performance, which may lead to various voice levels.

To cope with these adverse factors, the parameters of the recognition program have to be adjusted for performance optimization. For most application-oriented projects, we need to run the cognition program at the target hardware platform and verify its performance in realistic scenarios at different parameter values. The traditional design-implementation-validation loop is time-consuming, as it may involve a huge amount of coding and recoding. Automatic code generation and adjusting parameters on the fly are the promising features of the BeagleBoard rapid prototyping, which not only allow us to reduce the development time, but also enable us to find the right parameter values easily for performance optimization and identify defects of our program at an early stage.

In our voice recognition example, it is worth considering adjusting the following parameters:

- The gain in the Normalize block. By default, the gain is 2/65536 to normalize the 16-bit integer in the range of [-1, 1]. However, depending on the sound-electronic conversion efficiency of the hardware and the volume of the voice, we may adjust the gain to achieve better results in normalization.

- The hit-crossing offset in the Hit Crossing block. This is the threshold of voice detection and segmentation. When the RMS power of the voice signal is over the hit-crossing offset, the signal is considered to be a valid voice rather than the background noise. As a result, it triggers the voice-recognition process. If the threshold is too low and the background noise level is higher, the recognition process can be triggered many times falsely.

- The delay amount in voice segmentation. This parameter affects how many samples before and after the detected threshold crossing is used for voice recognition.

- The threshold of decision making. The threshold of the switch in the **Recognition subsystem** has impacts on the false-recognition rate and the rejection rate. In most cases, it is tricky to find an appropriate threshold and get a good tradeoff between false recognition and missing recognition.

- The parameters in the recognition algorithm, such as the window function in feature extraction, the number of codewords in a codebook in VQ training (that is, parameter k in function `vqlbg()`), distance measurement in VQ pattern matching, and so on.

You can adjust the parameters offline and re-compile the model. A better way is adjusting parameters on the fly, as demonstrated in the Parametric Audio Equalizer example in *Chapter 4, Automatic Code Generation*. To do this, you define a variable in the MATLAB workspace and refer to this variable in the Simulink model. Once you've changed the value of the variable in the MATLAB workspace, use the command `set_param()` to make the change take effect immediately on the BeagleBoard.

Other things to try

So far, we have had two separate Simulink models for training and recognition, respectively. They work well for the purpose of algorithm development and validation.

In order to make a more practical system, it would be good if we integrated these two Simulink models into one. The Simulink model (`VocRcgBB_TrnRcg.mdl`) in this chapter's source folder provides of an example for this.

These models serve as a starting point for developing and prototyping a more advanced voice recognition system. There are a lot of things you can try to explore the advantages of BeagleBoard and rapid prototyping.

References

[Adams1990] Adams, Russ, Sourcebook of Automatic Identification and Data Collection, Van Nostrand Reinhold, New York, 1990.

Summary

This chapter demonstrates the rapid prototyping of a voice recognition system on the BeagleBoard, including RMS voice detection, VQ training, pattern matching, and decision making. The demo is designed to operate for single users, and may be used in multiuser applications. The program in the demo can be further extended for various applications, such as voice control and speaker authorization in smart home applications.

Another important task we performed was adjusting the parameters to optimize recognition performance. This provided us with an advanced tool to reduce the time spent on code development, validation, and optimization. It also enabled us to concentrate on our concept and the data processing algorithm, and avoid intensive coding.

Next, we will develop a video processing system on the BeagleBoard for motion detection.

7
Digital Video-Based
Motion Detection

Similar to the last few chapters, this chapter is a step-by-step tutorial on converting a low-cost USB web camera and the BeagleBoard into a motion detector. This goal will be achieved by developing an algorithm of tracking a moving object in a sequence of video frames.

This chapter covers the following topics:

- Video input: A USB Logitech C310 web camera
- Video acquisition: A software module in Simulink to access the video frame
- Motion detection algorithm: A video processing algorithm to identify and detect the moving target
- Parameter adjustment: How to configure the system parameter to achieve a better application effect

By the end of this chapter, you will have a valid prototype of a motion detection system, based on which you can develop a well-functioning home security, vision analysis, or traffic monitoring application. All the evaluations will be performed on the BeagleBoard, which is capable of doing onboard computation for this kind of video processing applications.

Video input: Digital camera hardware connection

There are two general ways to connect a digital camera to the BeagleBoard: the simple USB interface, and the camera connector. The latter connector was designed to be used with camera modules from Leopard Imaging (`https://www.leopardimaging.com`). However, in this chapter we will follow the first USB approach, using a USB-based web camera which is easy to obtain online. A list of supported USB cameras has been provided at `http://www.ideasonboard.org/uvc`. The Logitech C310 has been employed for this book (around $30 from Amazon).

Another advantage of the USB camera is easy connection. After you get the Logitech C310, you can simply open the package and insert the USB interface into the BeagleBoard. An example of physical connection has been provided in the following figure:

Video acquisition: Software driver

In *Chapter 5, Digital I/O and Serial Communication*, we discussed how to implement drivers for external devices. Similarly, the camera requires a driver as well. Nonetheless, the driver for a digital camera is usually much more complex than what we have done until now, and it may be worth another book to discuss how to implement such a driver. Thanks to the open-source community and MATLAB, the **Video for Linux 2 (V4L2)** API driver has been implemented for the BeagleBoard and is ready to use. Detailed information about V4L2 can be found at `http://linuxtv.org/downloads/v4l-dvb-apis`.

In this chapter we call the V4L2 driver directly to acquire the video stream from the Logitech C310 digital camera. As a benefit, we can focus on how to implement a motion detection algorithm based on existing video input.

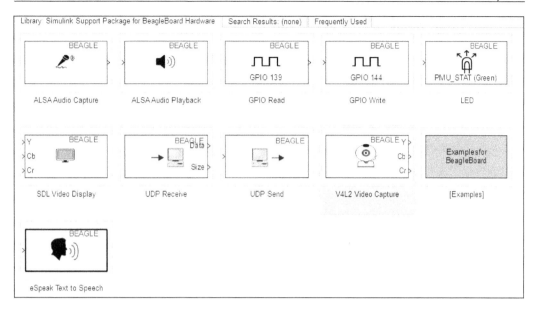

To obtain the video stream from the Logitech C310 camera, simply open the Simulink library and add a **V4L2 Video Capture** block (as shown in the previous screenshot) into our new model. Just like the audio data we discussed previously, the output of the **V4L2 Video Capture** block is frame data as well. At each sample time, the output data consists of three matrices corresponding to different color spaces. To make it easier to understand, we configured the V4L2 block into RGB mode and set the image size to **160*120** mode as shown in the following screenshot. Comparing with the default YCbCr color space, the RGB color space mode converts the captured video into three matrices, which represent the frame in red, green, and blue separately. These comprise the main data for processing in this motion detection algorithm.

Now let's drag an **SDL Video Display** block (the function of this block is very similar to the **Video Viewer** block, but utilizes the famous Simple DirectMedia Layer library to enable display on both a PC and a display screen connected to the BeagleBoard. Detailed information can be found at `http://www.libsdl.org/`) into our model and connect accordingly to form a minimized system of a video display application.

Additionally, a demonstration of the format of frame data can be achieved by dragging a **MATLAB Function** block from the user-defined functions section. As shown in the following screenshot, double-click on the icon and edit the function to `y=size(u)`. Then connect with a **Display** block to show the size of each frame from the **V4L2 Video Capture** block.

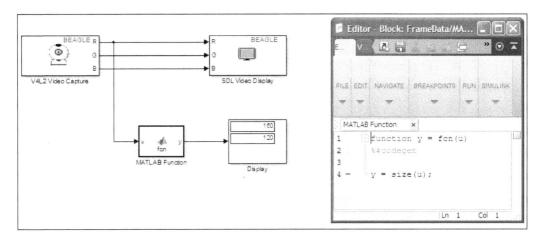

You can now deploy the model into the BeagleBoard to display the video stream. Navigate to **Tools** | **Run on Target hardware** | **Prepare to Run** to set up the necessary configurations following the discussion of early chapters. After the configuration, run the application through **Tools** | **Run on Target hardware** | **Run**. Then you can see that the green LED on the Logitech C310 is on, and a new **SDL** window pops out on your host PC's screen showing live video from the C310 camera.

There is a known issue with some types of cameras, which were reported to have dark points displayed. If you encounter this problem, try to avoid the direct use of a USB host interface on the BeagleBoard, and use the USB mini OTG interface (next to the 5V power interface) instead, with the aid of an OTG to USB adaptor (around $3 from eBay).

Motion detection algorithm

Now we have the video input ready to use and the video display working as well. The next step is the heart of this chapter: how to deploy a motion detection algorithm following the rapid prototype development principle.

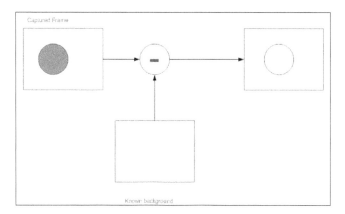

Firstly, let's spend some words to introduce the frame difference-based motion detection algorithm, which is employed in this chapter. As shown in the previous figure, the motivation is very simple. If we already know the background information — for example, if the background is stationary — then for each captured frame, simply subtracting the background image yields the regions of interest, that is, the motion area.

However, this method has several shortcomings. The most important is, how to get the background image? The best method is human aid. For example, the operator manually chooses a frame without any interesting object as the background image, which increases the operational complexity and uncertainty of the system. Even so, problems still exist in this approach. For example, lightweight leaves may swing in the wind and cause a false motion alarm. Similarly, the camera movement cannot be handled as well in this approach.

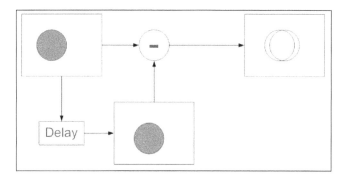

Therefore, researchers have proposed to use the frame differencing approach to increase the efficiency of motion detection, that is, calculate the different area between two adjacent frames as shown in the previous figure. Since we are utilizing the difference between adjacent frames, this approach is able to adapt to the changes caused by the camera and other unwanted movements. However, it should be noted that there are challenges in this method as well. The following figure shows an example of frame differencing results. The output of this algorithm only detects the leading and trailing edge of the moving objects. Since there are only a few pixels in the output and they are not closely connected, the detection algorithm is difficult to design, as shown in the following figure:

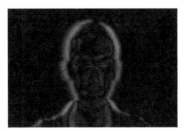

Simply increasing the number difference of two frames can increase the highlighted moving pixels, but may generate two copies of the object of interest. An example is shown in the following figure. Here comes the **three-frame difference** algorithm we employ in this chapter.

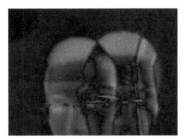

The basic idea is described in the following figure. Three frames are utilized as input information. The algorithm first calculates the difference between the first and second frames, followed by the difference between the second and third frames. As the following figure shows, the results of these two calculations have a shared area.

In detail, the first result (highlighted by a red circle, numbered 1) is the location of a moving object at both the first frame and the second frame, while the second result (highlighted by a red circle, numbered 2) is the location of a moving object at both the second frame and the third frame. By applying an AND operation (that is, find the shared area of two images) to these two temporal results, the output is the moving object in the second frame.

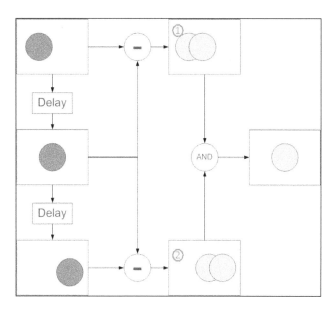

In this chapter, we employ the three-frame difference approach to detect the motion area of captured camera data. Based on the discussion of this chapter, it should be convenient to implement advanced algorithms such as **statistical background estimation**.

Implementation algorithm in Simulink

So far, we have explored the basic idea of a motion detection algorithm. In this section, we show how to detail and implement this algorithm in Simulink, and deploy it to the BeagleBoard step by step.

Grayscale image

The first issue is regarding the color space. Since a frame with RGB color space contains redundant information in three colors, we implement the motion detector algorithm in monochrome to save computation cost. We first convert the frame data from RGB color space into the grayscale format with the **Color Space Conversion** block, which can be found in the **Computer Vision System** toolbox. Let's drag this **Color Space Conversion** block into our minimum system, and double-click on the icon to configure the conversion mode into RGB to intensity mode and the image signal into separate color signals through the dropdown selection. After the processing of this block, the frame data has been converted from [160,120,3] into a simpler two-dimension matrix [160,120].

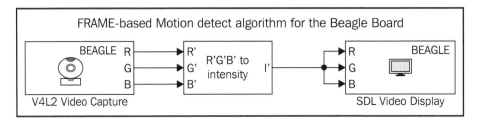

It should be noted that, unlike the common **Video Viewer** block, the **SDL Video Display** block cannot automatically recognize the format of input signals. Therefore, we need to manually connect the intensity output to all the three ports (R, G, and B) of the **SDL Video Display** block. The connection scheme has been provided in the previous figure, while a sample output of the grayscale frame, rather than the color output, has been provided in the following figure:

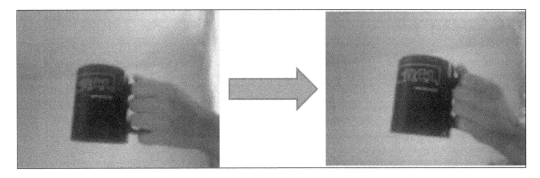

Since we have got the raw material for implementation of the algorithm, the next step is the delay of the frame to get **Three Frames**. This can be done with the help of the **Delay** block from the Simulink/commonly used block section. Simply drag a **Delay** block into the model (between the **Computer Vision System** block and the **SDL Video Display** block), then deploy it to the BeagleBoard to see the delay effect. To check how the video is delayed by the **Delay** block, simply run the revised program and move an object in front of the camera; you can notice the replayed video is slightly lagging behind your actual movement. To highlight the effect, you may double-click on the **Delay** block and increase the delay length, to say 5.

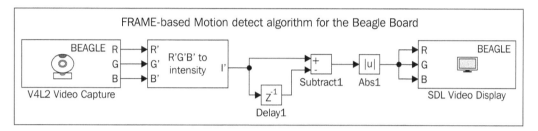

Nevertheless, the delay of the frame is not the target. What we really need is to utilize the delay function to get the difference between frames. By this point of time, we have already got the original frame and the delayed frame. With additional aid from the **Subtract** block and **Abs** block, we should get the frame difference result. As shown in the previous screenshot, we connect these Simulink blocks and send the result to the display.

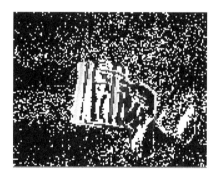

Surprisingly, the output result is not as good as we expected. An example has been shown in the previous figure, which is extremely noisy. Here we are wondering how this noise comes. Considering the original video is of high quality, this noise has a very low probability of being caused by the hardware device.

Unlike the Simulink model running in the PC, this model has been compiled and downloaded onto the BeagleBoard. Running programs on an embedded system usually has an integer-width problem. Since the output of the V4L2 driver is uint8 (that is, unsigned integer 8-bit), then the **Subtract** block will automatically set to uint8. Then the subtracting operation may cause this problem. For example, the first pixel in the first frame is 4, while the first pixel in the second frame is 5. The **Subtract** block output in the PC will be -1. Then the output in the BeagleBoard is 254 if implemented with the uint8 subtract operation. These large numbers contribute to the high-energy noise pixels, which should be a low-energy pixel (that is, almost zero).

To solve this uint8 subtract problem, we must manually configure the data type of the **Subtract** block into **int32** as shown in the following screenshot. This can easily fix the mentioned problem, since the data type is signed integer with 32-bit width (that is, 4 minus 5 will result in -1). Then we need an additional **Data Type Conversion** block to change the data type back to uint8 for the SDL display.

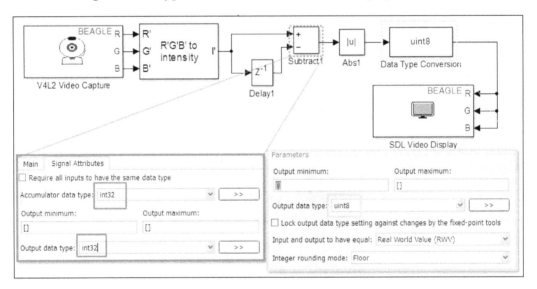

After this modification, here we can see the ideal result, or more exactly the correct output, in the following figure. The noise pixels disappeared, and the edge of the moving object has been highlighted, which has been discussed in the last section.

Now we have got the difference result of the first two frames. A simple copy (highlighted by a red circle, numbered 1 in the following screenshot) and paste gives us the difference between the second and third frames. At this time, let's try the delay length of 2 for both calculations, which means the algorithm is implemented based on the current - 2 and current - 4 frames.

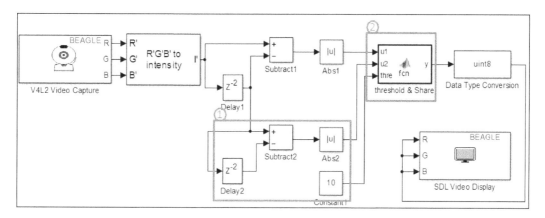

Then the next step is the three-frame difference algorithm that we discussed in the last section. The main tasks of this algorithm, that is, converting the frame into a binary image and calculating the shared pixels as output, are too complex to find suitable Simulink blocks to implement. As a result, we deploy this algorithm in a **MATLAB Function** block through m-language.

Similarly to what we have done earlier in this chapter to get the size of the frame, we drag a **MATLAB Function** block into the model (highlighted by a red circle, numbered 2 in the previous screenshot). We can edit the function of this block by double-clicking on the icon (you may refer to the previous chapter for detailed information). As shown in the following code, let's firstly modify the function input to assign two more parameters, u2 and thre. After saving the function, the input port number of the **MATLAB Function** block shown in the Simulink GUI changes to three with a specified name. The u1 port is the input for the difference result of the first and second frames, while the u2 port is the input for the difference result of the second and third frames. The third port thre is used to specify the threshold to convert the grayscale frame into a binary frame (that is, all the pixels should be either 0 or 255).

```
function y = fcn(u1,u2,thre)
%#codegen
[I,J]=size(u1);
T=zeros(I,J);

for i=1:I
  for j=1:J
    %use threshold to convert frame into BW format
    if u1(i,j)>thre
      U1=255;
    else
      U1=0;
    end

    if u2(i,j)>thre
      U2=255;
    else
      U2=0;
    end

    %calculate the share part between two input frame difference
    if U1==255 && U2==255
      T(i,j)=255;
    else
      T(i,j)=0;
    end
  end
end
%output
y = T;
```

The code of the **MATLAB Function** block has been provided previously. The first-half of the code utilized the input parameter `thre` to convert the grayscale frame into a binary frame by comparing the value of each pixel with the threshold. Then a simple algorithm has been implemented to select the pixels as output, if they existed in both of the results of frames difference (that is, the shared area).

The output result of the previous model running on the BeagleBoard is similar to the example shown in the previous figure, where not only the edges, but also the whole moving object has been highlighted.

Image enhancement

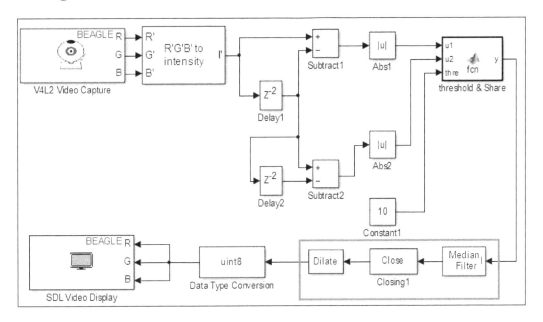

This rough result until now is fine enough to be utilized to detect the motion area. However, to make the detection process simpler, we can deploy several normal image-processing functions to emphasize the area. The following three blocks in the **Computer Vision System Toolbox** are employed as shown in the previous screenshot:

- The **Median Filter** block filters the distributed small noise pixels
- The **Close** block performs a morphological closing operation
- The **Dilate** block performs a morphological dilation operation

The **Close** block and the **Dilate** block have been employed here to enlarge the recognized moving object. The effect of these imaging processing functions has been provided in the following figure. It's easy to see that , this result is easier to process as compared with the raw results.

Detection of the moving area

Now that everything is ready for the motion detection, what we need to do is just highlight the "white" area. The basic algorithm is scanning the image from the upper-left corner, and recording the first non-zero point as well as the last point in the lower-right corner. We can then draw a bounding box to highlight the moving object using these two location points. This function has been provided through the **Blob Analysis** block in the **Computer Vision System Toolbox**. The **Blob Analysis** block (highlighted by a red box, numbered 1 in the following screenshot) uses the output image from the **Dilate** block and calculates the connected area. The analyses results are outputted as bounding-box locations, that is, the location of the upper-left point and the width and height. It should be noted that the **Blob Analysis** block requires a binary frame as input, so we need to set the data type conversion to `Boolean` mode, rather than `uint8` mode.

To work with the **Blob Analysis** block, the **Draw Rectangles** block (highlighted by a red circle, numbered 2) takes the output of the **Blob Analysis** block and the raw video frame as input. The output is the raw frame with several highlighted boxes to show the detected motion area. The final model has been provided in the following screenshot. For your convenience, a ready-to-use Simulink model `MotionDetectBeagle.slx` has been enclosed in the code folder as well.

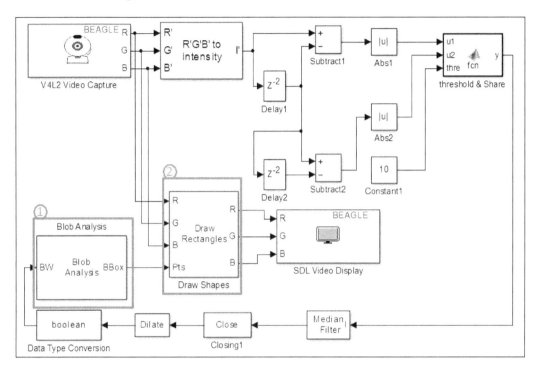

You can now try to deploy the model onto the BeagleBoard. You may need to wait a few seconds for the compiling and downloading processes. During this period, adjust the direction of your camera to an open area. And when the downloading process is finished, walk in front of the BeagleBoard. The output window automatically draws a box of your body in the frame.

Congratulations, you have now built a well-functioning video-based motion detection algorithm. If you wish, you can add more functions, for example, to flash the LED in the BeagleBoard as soon as a motion area has been detected. In fact, you can extend any function to this system as you wish to explore the advantages of BeagleBoard and rapid prototyping.

Parameter optimization

As we discussed earlier in this chapter, the effect and accuracy of the three-frame difference algorithm are highly correlated with the parameter chosen. Theoretically, we can analyze the optimized parameter for a given system. However, in real-life system design, the best configuration of a system parameter is more or less an experience value. Therefore, in the prototype design process, we usually have to frequently adjust the parameter and check the output to find the best solution.

In this system, there are two parameters closely related to system performance. The first is the delay length of three frames, and the second is the threshold value to convert a frame into a binary image. The threshold is already a parameter input configured with a **Constant** block. Here we set the delay length of the **Delay** block with a configurable input port as well. You can simply double-click on the **Delay** block and set the source of delay length into the input port, and then drag another **Constant** block and connect it with these input ports. The connection scheme has been provided in the following screenshot:

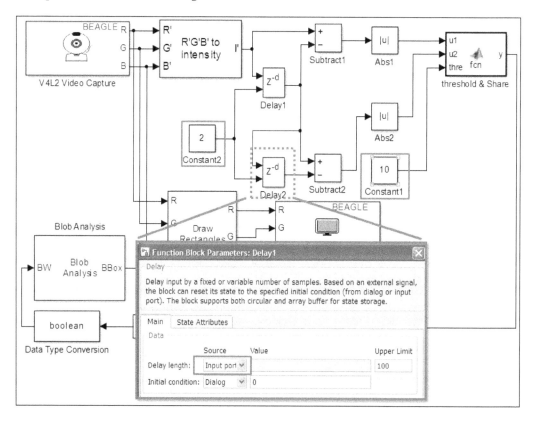

Now, we can easily change the value in offline or on the fly fashion (as demonstrated in the parametric audio equalizer example in *Chapter 4, Automatic Code Generation*). You may want to try and find the best parameter for your system.

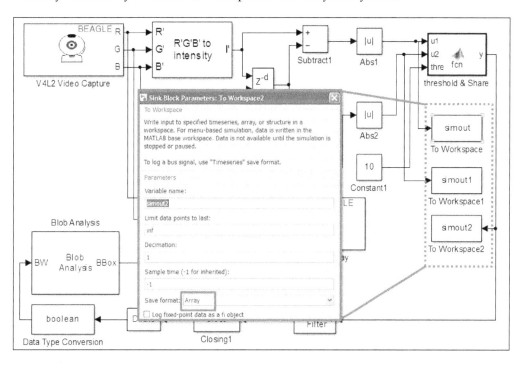

We just mentioned that another approach is theoretical optimization. This approach is also very important and widely employed. Although the theoretical calculation is disturbed by many noise inputs, it can still narrow the candidate area, which can significantly save time and computational costs. This method usually requires a deep understanding of the system and mathematical analyses. We may not discuss an optimization process for this computer vision application, since it is beyond the scope of this book. Instead we provide you with the necessary tools to carry out this process. Generally, this kind of optimization process requires massive source data and offline calculation. To satisfy it, we can drag the **Save to Workspace** block into different stages of the model. Since the data stream is a frame-based value, we configure the save format into **Array** instead of a **Time** series (as shown in the previous screenshot). After the system has been deployed onto the BeagleBoard, three variables are added into the MATLAB workspace. You may carry out any analyses and optimization based on these data, which can guide your parameter optimization process. For example, the best value of threshold to binarize the image under certain scenarios can be obtained by following this approach. By saving massive frames of input into an array in the MATLAB workspace, we can do statistical analyses on these frames and calculate the optimized value for the current scenario.

Summary

In this chapter, we went slightly further on the basis of the last few chapters to explore a video-based application on the BeagleBoard. In detail, a step-by-step tutorial was given to demonstrate how to design a motion detection application by using a low-cost USB web camera and Simulink-based rapid prototype design. The program developed in this chapter can be directly applied to many video applications, such as home security, traffic monitoring, and so on.

Wrapping Up

Throughout the previous chapters, we have looked at various tools and technologies for BeagleBoard rapid prototyping. We covered various projects and examples, from simple data processing, music file reading by S-function block, digital I/O access, serial communication, voice recognition to video processing, all of which have been demonstrated and explained for understanding the concept and workflow of MATLAB/Simulink automatic code generation for BeagleBoard.

In this chapter, we will review what we have learned and then look at how you can grow your skills and start to prototype your own BeagleBoard project.

A brief review of what we have learned

We started off with an introduction to BeagleBoard for new users, followed by the concept of MATLAB and Simulink rapid prototyping.

In *Chapter 2*, *Installing Linux on the BeagleBoard*, we set up the BeagleBoard target system and configured a Windows 7 PC as a host PC for cross-platform development. *Chapter 3*, *C/C++ Development with Eclipse on Windows* demonstrated how to build our first program, a classic Hello World! on the Windows 7 host PC. The key feature of our development is the pure Windows-based cross-platform compiler CodeBench Lite. Two embedded code generation methods for rapid prototyping, namely, textual programming in MATLAB, and graphical programming in Simulink were discussed in *Chapter 4*, *Automatic Code Generation*. They were demonstrated by two projects: a MATLAB program for an averaging operation, and a Simulink model of a music player. One unique feature of Simulink prototyping is the performance optimization by tuning parameters on the fly. In the last three chapters, various applications from simple digital I/O access, serial communication, IR sensor with motion detection, voice recognition to advanced video motion detection are developed, which demonstrate the features and advantages of MATLAB/Simulink rapid prototyping.

We slowly built up a set of rapid prototyping techniques covering from simple data processing to advanced video processing. These techniques and algorithms are transferable to devices that have different applications, for example, home security, biometric identification, and traffic monitoring.

We can now use these methods and techniques to build custom applications, which we will look at now.

Ideas for next-step projects

Armed with the knowledge and skills of rapid prototyping, you are now able to create exciting new applications to realize your unique ideas quickly.

Expanding the IR motion detector to include verbal alarms

We developed a music player in *Chapter 4*, *Automatic Code Generation*, and motion detection via the IR sensor in *Chapter 5*, *Digital I/O and Serial Communication*. We can now try combining them together to give verbal alarms when a motion is detected. If we have multiple IR sensors in different rooms, we may have the BeagleBoard speak out to tell us in which room a motion is detected.

Voice-controlled light switch

In *Chapter 5*, *Digital I/O and Serial Communication*, we learned how to control a digital I/O, and in *Chapter 6*, *Voice Recognition*, we learned how to switch on the user LED on a BeagleBoard by voice recognition. Controlling an LED was easy enough, but a table lamp requires high currents and voltages. With the extension board xM-Trainer (as shown in *Chapter 5*, *Digital I/O and Serial Communication*), we can build an additional power control circuit that controls high currents and voltages (that is, 230 V main supply to the table lamp) through a low voltage signal (that is, the GPIO output). Building such a power control switch is demonstrated at `www.sparkfun.com/tutorials/119`. The core of the switch is a silicon-controlled switch (SCS, or referred to as **thyristor**) or a relay. A good introduction to relays can be found at `www.electronics-tutorials.ws/io/io_5.html`, and you can buy a cheap single-channel relay for power control on sparkfun. Then replacing the **LED** block with a **GPIO Write** block in our voice recognition example, and connecting the GPIO to your power control switch, you will get a voice-controlled light switch.

Voice biometric authentication systems

Another application of the voice recognition system we developed in *Chapter 6, Voice Recognition* is speaker identification. This provides us with the technology to make a voice authentication system. The core of voice processing is almost ready; what you need is a better user interface for training and device controlling (for example, a magnetic switch controlling a door). Using voice biometrics to authenticate a person through natural voice patterns, not robotic PINs, passwords, and questions is a brand new user experience.

2D Ball tracking

For advanced image processing, tracking a ball (such as the Hawk-Eye system used in cricket, tennis, football, and so on) is an interesting task to start with. Hawk-Eye is an advanced commercial system for 3D tracking. It is too complicated and expensive, but we can start with a simple 2D ball tracking. We may find a lot of video processing algorithms at MATLAB **File Exchange** (www.mathworks. com/matlabcentral/fileexchange/) for free, and you can evaluate their performances using real hardware. A good example is the Kalman Filter demo for Ball Tracking (www.mathworks.com/matlabcentral/fileexchange/42257- kalman-filter-demo-for-ball-tracking). The demo of C code generation for a MATLAB Kalman Filtering Algorithm (www.mathworks.com/help/coder/ examples/c-code-generation-for-a-matlab-kalman-filtering-algorithm. html?prodcode=ME&language=en) would be helpful for implementing the Kalman filter on a BeagleBoard.

Gesture-controlled devices

Other interesting video applications of object tracking would be hand tracking and gesture control. Hewlett-Packard recently introduced a laptop with a built-in sensor that lets users control the onscreen action with hand gestures. You may create your own gesture control for your BeagleBoard. The *Virtual Touch Screen* project and *American Sign Language Detection using PCA and LDA* are freely available on MATLAB **File Exchange**. By integrating the source code of the aforementioned projects into your BeagleBoard rapid prototyping project, it is much easier and quicker to have your own gesture control system on your BeagleBoard.

Useful references and websites

The BeagleBoard is an inexpensive single-board computer with a lot of potential. The MATLAB/Simulink rapid prototyping techniques reduce the burden of embedded software development. By combining these two technologies, we have got a fantastic tool to realize your unique ideas.

In this book, we have been aiming to provide you with examples that are useful and give you a good starting point for your advanced systems. The BeagleBoard and MATLAB communities are growing faster by the day, and the best place to find related projects, ideas, and solutions are on their community websites and forums, such as:

- BeagleBoard home page: `http://beagleboard.org/`
- BeagleBoard-xM reference manual and CircuitCo support: `circuitco.com/support/index.php?title=BeagleBoard-xM`
- BeagleBoard Projects: `http://beagleboard.org/project/`
- MATLAB **File Exchange**: `http://www.mathworks.com/matlabcentral/fileexchange/`
- BeagleBoard code sharing: `https://code.google.com/p/beagleboard/`
- BeagleBoard Google Group: `https://groups.google.com/forum/#!forum/beagleboard`
- BeagleBoard Support from Simulink: `www.mathworks.com/hardware-support/beagleboard.html`
- **MATLAB and Simulink Student version** FAQ: `http://www.mathworks.com/academia/student_version/faq/`
- SparkFun Electronics for buying peripheral device `https://www.sparkfun.com/`
- Touchscreen by CircuitCo for BeagleBoard: `beagleboardtoys.info/index.php?title=BeagleBoard-xM_LCD7`

With the information in this book and on the Internet, it is now over to you to continue your journey with BeagleBoard and MATLAB/Simulink rapid prototyping.

Index

D

decision-making block 93
digital audio signals 89
digital camera hardware connection 110
digital I/O
  used, for interfacing sensors in
    Simulink 73-75
digital signal processing (DSP) systems 91
digital video-based motion detector
  motion detection algorithm 113, 114
  motion detection algorithm, implementing
    in Simulink 115
  parameter optimization 124, 125
  video acquisition 110
  video input 110
driver 70
Dynamic Time Warping (DTW) 99

E

Eclipse IDE
  about 54
  BeagleBoard, connecting to RSE 38, 39
  GNU ARM Eclipse plugin, installing 35
  installing, on Windows 7 35
  Remote System Explorer (RSE),
    installing 36
Eclipse project
  creating, for BeagleBoard
    applications 54, 55
executable
  running, at BeagleBoard 55

F

feature extraction 93
FFT 95
frame-based signal processing, in Simulink 90
  about 90
  benefits 91
frame-blocking 94

G

gesture-controlled device 129
GNU ARM Eclipse plugin
  installing 35

G (right column)

GPIO Write 89
graphic user interfaces (GUIs) 66

H

Hamming window 95
hardware setup, BeagleBoard
  components, connecting 15
  compulsory hardware 14
  hardware, for rapid prototyping 15
Hello World! program
  building 40
  C/C++ Build, configuring 41, 42
  compiling 43, 44
  creating, in Eclipse 40
  cross-compiler, configuring 41
  program files, transferring to
    Beagleboard 44
  remote debugging 46
  remote debugging, with Eclipse 45
  running, at Beagleboard 45
  running, with Eclipse 45, 46
Hidden Markov Modeling (HMM) 99

I

IR motion detector
  2D Ball tracking 129
  expanding 128
  gesture-controlled device 129
  voice biometric authentication systems 129
  voice-controlled light switch 128
IR sensor hardware 70
  analog interface 71
  connecting, to BeagleBoard 70
  serial communication interface 71
  ZMotion 70

L

Linde-Buzo-Gray (LBG) algorithm 99
Linux operating system. *See* Ubuntu

M

MathWorks
  about 12
  URL 21

W

Win32 Disk Imager
  used, for creating microSD cards 29
Windows 7
  Eclipse IDE, installing 35
Windows 7 PC
  software, installing 16
  Ubuntu, installing 23
Windows-based cross-complier 32
window weighting 95

Z

ZMotion IR sensor
  about 70, 71
  analog interface 71
  connecting, to BeagleBoard 71, 72
  serial communication interface 71
  voltage shifting 72

About Packt Publishing

Packt, pronounced 'packed', published its first book *"Mastering phpMyAdmin for Effective MySQL Management"* in April 2004 and subsequently continued to specialize in publishing highly focused books on specific technologies and solutions.

Our books and publications share the experiences of your fellow IT professionals in adapting and customizing today's systems, applications, and frameworks. Our solution based books give you the knowledge and power to customize the software and technologies you're using to get the job done. Packt books are more specific and less general than the IT books you have seen in the past. Our unique business model allows us to bring you more focused information, giving you more of what you need to know, and less of what you don't.

Packt is a modern, yet unique publishing company, which focuses on producing quality, cutting-edge books for communities of developers, administrators, and newbies alike. For more information, please visit our website: www.packtpub.com.

Writing for Packt

We welcome all inquiries from people who are interested in authoring. Book proposals should be sent to author@packtpub.com. If your book idea is still at an early stage and you would like to discuss it first before writing a formal book proposal, contact us; one of our commissioning editors will get in touch with you.

We're not just looking for published authors; if you have strong technical skills but no writing experience, our experienced editors can help you develop a writing career, or simply get some additional reward for your expertise.

MATLAB Graphics and Data Visualization Cookbook

ISBN: 978-1-84969-316-5   Paperback: 284 pages

Tell data stories with compelling graphics using this collection of data visualization recipes

1. Collection of data visualization recipes with functionalized versions of common tasks for easy integration into your data analysis workflow

2. Recipes cross-referenced with MATLAB product pages and MATLAB Central File Exchange resources for improved coverage

Visual Media Processing Using MATLAB Beginner's Guide

ISBN: 978-1-84969-720-0   Paperback: 334 pages

Learn range of techniques from enhancing and adding artistic effects of your photographs, to editing and processing your videos, all using MATLAB

1. Apply sophisticated techniques to images and videos in just a few steps

2. Learn and practice techniques for enhancing and restoring your photographs

3. Create artistic photographs using simple methods

Please check **www.PacktPub.com** for information on our titles

Scratch 1.4 Beginner's Guide

ISBN: 978-1-84719-676-7   Paperback: 264 pages

Learn to program while creating interactive stories, games, and multimedia projects using Scratch

1. Create interactive stories, games, and multimedia projects that you can reuse in your own classroom

2. Learn computer programming basics – no computer science degree required

3. Connect with the Scratch community for inspiration, advice, and collaboration

Instant RubyMotion App Development [Instant]

ISBN: 978-1-84969-652-4   Paperback: 54 pages

A jump start to quickly learn how to program iOS applications witht the elegance and simplicity of Ruby

1. Learn something new in an Instant! A short, fast, focused guide delivering immediate results

2. Learn the structure of iPhone and iPad applications

3. Discover how to simplify iOS apps with Ruby

4. Get to grips with how to leverage Ruby libraries to quickly and efficiently write apps!

Please check **www.PacktPub.com** for information on our titles

www.ingramcontent.com/pod-product-compliance
Lightning Source LLC
LaVergne TN
LVHW080058070326
832902LV00014B/2303